How to Help, Not Harm

First published in 2018 by Orphanage Projects
www.orphanageprojects.org
ISBN 978-0-9935023-3-0

Layout and cover design by Bert Koenderink
Illustration on the cover by Jess Fogel
Editing by Willow Editing

How to Help, Not Harm

What Living in Orphanages Does to Children, and How You Can Help

Florence Koenderink

Other books by Florence Koenderink

Children Everywhere Book 1:
Essential Elements of Childcare in Institutions
(2nd edition 2017)

Sick Children Everywhere Book 2:
Basic Medical Care for Children in Institutions

Volunteering with Children Everywhere
Book 3: *Manual for Volunteers in Children's Homes*

Dedicated to
all the children I have met in institutions
who did not survive

Acknowledgements

The insights discussed in this book have been gathered and built over the course of more than ten years of visiting and working inside children's homes. Even though, as you will find out, many of the lessons I have learned and the things I have seen were not pleasant, they were useful and necessary. For that, I want to thank all the people I have met and worked alongside in children's homes over the years. Both those who are doing their utmost, to the best of their knowledge, to offer the children in their care a better life, and those who allowed me to witness the realities of substandard care and to better understand the darker side of the orphanage industry by seeing it in action. I want to thank all of the institutionalised children who helped me gain a deeper understanding of the terrible consequences of institutional childcare. Seeing the lives these children lead compels me to keep fighting to improve their situation by doing things like writing this book, to help other people understand what is going on.

I would also like to thank Léa Guillamot and Yana Bogomolova for reading an early draft and providing me with feedback to make the content clearer and more digestible. As always, I want to thank Bert Koenderink for doing an amazing job on the cover design and the layout. Jess Fogel for the wonderful illustration she made for the cover of this book. And Elzevera Koenderink for cleaning up the text after me, once again.

My motto remains: I cannot change the world, but I can change the world for one child. And then another. And another…And so can you!

How Could Donating to an Orphanage Do Harm?

Most of us very much want to do something to help the weakest among us, those who are most vulnerable. We feel a moral obligation to help improve the lives of those who are unable to help themselves. And we feel a sense of satisfaction and contentment when we think that a small sacrifice on our part will improve the quality of life of those less fortunate. From ancient times, the moral obligation and the command to take care of widows and orphans has been heard across different cultures and different religions.

This sense of obligation is commendable. We *should* do what we can to help those who need help. We *should* recognise that these are people who need help–regardless of their nationality, religion, or political opinion–and that at some point we, or our parents, our children or our friends, could end up in the same unfortunate position through no fault of our own. The desire to help is not the problem. The problem lies in knowing the difference between what would truly help those in need and what might end up harming them. We do not like to think that the sacrifice or the kind, generous gesture that we have made might do more harm than good. But it would be irresponsible not to consider the possibility if we are serious about wanting to help.

The potential to do more harm than good exists in all forms of charitable help and developmental aid. The proof of that can be found in the serious harm and in some cases death and destruction as a result of well-meaning but ill-informed 'charitable aid' given in many developing countries over the past century and more. An example is the introduction of the European notion of institutional childcare across the world.[1] Tackling the entire subject of the-potential-harm caused by charitable and developmental aid would go beyond my field of knowledge. Instead, in this book, I want to focus on one tiny aspect of it: the potential harm of sponsoring so-called orphanages, something I am quite familiar with.

Over the past ten years, I have visited dozens of orphanages and children's homes in five different countries all across the world. Through my NGO, Orphanage Projects–which consists of me, a website, a Facebook page and a series of manuals–I have worked alongside caregivers inside various children's homes. I have analysed the care-system, have given advice and training, and generally have helped the management to improve the children's chances of survival and their quality of life. Through both my experience inside children's homes and the research I have done surrounding it, I have developed a thorough understanding of institutional childcare and its effects on children. By giving you a look into some of the things I have seen along the way, combined with the knowledge of other experts and researchers, I will try to provide an insight in the realities of children living in children's homes.

The reason I do this work has never been that I thought children would be better off in children's homes, as a lot of people still do–in the second chapter, I will explain why they are in fact not better off there. However, initially, I did think that there was no alternative to institutional childcare in many places. I believed, as many people still do today, that if these children would not be in these children's homes, they would be worse off, possibly dying by the side of the road. I welcomed the great work done by UNICEF and other major organisations that try to put an end to institutionalisation. However, most of those organisations focus on creating circumstances that slow down and eventually prevent the arrival of new children into children's homes. This is good news for the next generation of children, but I rather resented the way the current generation of children in children's homes–an estimated 8 million of them across the globe[2] –seemed to be forgotten. I did not want to allow that generation of children to waste away in these places, just because we would prefer they were not there. There are very few organisations that actively work to move children currently living in children's homes into better situations. While I want to see the end of institutional childcare, I am unable to bring that about right now. So for the time being I have focused on somewhat improving conditions inside children's home, something that was within my reach.

I have never given money to children's homes, although I was asked for it almost without exception. One reason for this was that I do not really have any money beyond what I earn to keep myself alive. But it was also because I noticed quite early on that not providing money was a very good way of finding out whether a children's home was actually interested in improving the conditions for their children, or whether they were merely looking for a milking cow: the coveted foreign donor.

I regularly receive emails asking me to help an orphanage. I always reply saying that I am most happy to help in any way I can, but that I cannot and will not give them money. In seven to eight out of ten cases, that is the last I ever hear from them. There was the place in Honduras that persisted and asked me for advice on how to have the children bring in more money, I refused to give advice on that.

Out of the remaining places–after they have assured me that they understand I will not bring in money and they would like me to visit their children's home to give them advice on how to improve things for the children–some are still really only looking for money. They hope that once I have seen the 'poor,

poor children' and once they have been able to tell me their sad stories of sacrifice and deprivation, I will be convinced to pay up after all, or that I will want to find other people to pay them. These are places I only visit once or twice, because it soon becomes clear that I will not be able to make any improvements for the children there. That only leaves a tiny percentage of places that really are looking for guidance and that really have the desire to do as well as they can for the children using the resources and knowledge available. These are the places that slowly but surely improve over the years. Despite these improvements, however, the children are still not well off in these places. Even in the ones that are incredibly well-run–relatively speaking–children still show clear signs of physical and cognitive developmental delays and behavioural problems, which worsen as the years progress.

It is through encountering the limits of the kind of care that can be provided in an institution and by seeing how the best children's homes are not good enough[3] and how the worst children's homes provide a fate that could be seen as worse than dying by the side of the road–which would be quick, rather than prolonged suffering–that I have gradually become more vocal in pushing for deinstitutionalisation and that I have started to dedicate part of my time to preventing children from ending up in children's homes. This book is part of that effort.

To give you some of idea of what I am talking

about, I would like to share my first impressions of the first time I visited an extremely bad children's home. These words hardly scrape the surface of what the situation was like, but I think it is important to make an attempt to give an impression of the circumstances anyway.

> There are three rooms, 12 cots in a room, side by side, with just enough room in-between to stand sideways. Over the sides of the cots, wet children's clothes are hanging to dry. The overwhelming smell of urine, with lower undertones of mould and dirt is almost tangible. It wraps itself around you as soon as you set foot inside. Not even the weak human sense of smell, which so quickly phases out odours to the background, is able to ignore this, not even after an hour or more.
>
> In most of the cots lie babies, or so they are called. The youngest is about a month old, but the oldest might well be two or three years old. It is very hard to say. Growth and development are all stunted. Almost all are lying down, unable to sit or stand. Or perhaps they have learned that anything other than lying quietly is undesirable. Almost all those over the age of ten months lie rocking back and forth. Their head, or their entire body if they are not sleeping. Sores on their heads from banging against the bars of the cot. Some with their faces pressed against the bars, their neck at an uncomfortable angle. One little boy grates the paint off the bed with his teeth.
>
> The room is very cold–and it is not yet winter, autumn has only just started. The children all wear clothes, but no socks, and only the smallest are covered by a blanket

or a quilt. All hands and feet are cold. One little boy's feet are dark purple and icy. Clothes, bed linen, children, everything is dirty.

A boy with sores on his nose and eyes. A child of maybe two years old, able to stand, has a string tied around his leg, the other side of which is tied around one of the bars of his bed. All children, without exception, have bottoms covered in big sores, blisters, purplish spots and sometimes even big open wounds, which keep reopening. Not only on their buttocks, but also on their genitalia. All from lying in their own urine and faeces. Sores on heels are common, as are heads flattened at the back from always lying on them.

A lot of the children have given up reacting to touch or being spoken to. Others are still desperate to make contact. From the moment you enter the room, they will not stop crying or saying the one word they know. All children are hungry; when you stroke a cheek–even of children too old to have a rooting reflex–the face will invariably turn with a desperately opened mouth looking for something, anything, to eat.

A remark made about one baby being dehydrated and another having a perforated middle ear infection–observations made at a glance by someone without a medical background–are received with surprise by caregivers, who had not noticed. A baby who is weak has no chance of survival. You need to be able to drink well and fast, on your own, otherwise the propped-up bottle will have been removed and you will have to wait for the next round.

In the rooms, there is not so much as a stool to sit on while holding a child. There is no need for it. There is no time for holding children. One caregiver looks after 10 to 20 children. Not only is she responsible for feeding and changing the babies, she also has to hand-wash all their clothes and bedding. She barely has enough time to make the babies' bottles, prop them up, take them away, and from time to time change nappies–rags tied around waists. There is no time or energy to try and do more than get through the day. Is it days, weeks, or months since the baby was last picked up out of his bed?

Food is for those who can take it. Upstairs with the older children–three years and older–it is lunchtime. In the corridor, there is a bucket with food and a stack of bowls next to it. The children can help themselves. If they don't–be it because they are too small to understand or because they are mentally handicapped–well, maybe next time.

Witnessing a situation like this for the first time is like a punch to the stomach. It is unimaginable. As I got to know this particular place better, I was not very surprised to find out that babies regularly died there. I have seen places like this more often over the years, but this was the first one to confront me with the reality and the effects of minimal care. In places like these, there is just enough care to prolong lives, but not enough to give much chance of actual survival. Meaning that essentially, only more suffering is provided.

Over the past three pages you have gotten a general idea of how I accumulated the knowledge I have about institutional childcare and its effect on children, and the reason I am more and more becoming an advocate for deinstitutionalisation. In a practical sense, I try to tackle the institutional childcare problem on two levels:

- For the projects in various children's homes that I am involved in, I suggest ways of reuniting children with their family, of finding foster homes for them, of starting community projects that will help parents take care of their own children or–if all else fails–of setting up a family-like group home system, instead of the more popular and absolutely detrimental traditional orphanage setup with large dorms and few caregivers.
- For people who encourage the existence of children's homes by providing them with money, I write this book to explain what happens with and because of that money.

Now that my part in all of this has been established, let's get back to the topic at hand: What could possibly be wrong with helping an orphanage? To get to the bottom of this, we have to start with the misleading term 'orphanage'. Using the word 'orphanages' makes it sound like they are filled with children who have lost their parents and who have no one to care for them. In fact, 80 to 90%–in some cases even more than 90%–of children in so-called orphanages have at least one living parent.[4] Many of them even have two living parents. This is why I only use the word 'orphanage' between quotation marks and prefer to speak of children's homes, a more accurate term.

UNICEF calculated that in 2005, there were 132 million single and full orphans–meaning children who have lost at least one parent–in sub-Saharan Africa, Asia, Latin America, and the Caribbean, the areas where institutional childcare is most prevalent. Of those 132 million only 13 million had lost both parents. UNICEF also states that evidence shows that the vast majority of single and full orphans live with a surviving parent, grandparent or other family member.[5] This is illustrated by the fact that out of an estimated 8 million children in children's homes[6] less than 10 to 20% are full orphans. So clearly, so-called orphanages are not all that essential for making sure that orphans have a home. The proof of this lies in the fact that only a small fraction of real, full, orphans end up in 'orphanages'.

This raises the question: if 'orphanages' are not full of orphans, who do live there? There are many reasons for children to end up in children's homes, but the top ones are poverty,[7] special needs and education.[8] Education, in this context, splits up into four branches, which overlap with poverty and special needs:[9]

- Poverty: When a family is unable to afford school fees, books, uniforms and transport to school, they may realise how important education is, and want to provide it, but be unable to do so for their children.
- Presence of schools within a distance that can be travelled daily: In some remote rural areas, there may quite simply not be any school within half a day's walking distance.
- Minority background: Children who come from an ethnic or religious minority background, particularly if that minority is repressed in their country, may not be admitted to regular schools, depriving them of their right to education.[10]
- Special needs: Mainstream schools may refuse to accept children with severe physical and any type of cognitive impairment, while special education facilities are often rare and therefore not necessarily available within a distance that can be travelled.[11]

Parents or family members who do not know how to feed their children and keep them warm, who are unable to give their children an education and who are unable to afford the medical bills or the special equipment needed by their child with special needs often feel that they have no choice but to give up their child to a children's home.[12] In most cases, children are abandoned not because their parents do not care about them, but as an act of sacrifice, hoping to give them a better future.[13] In the fourth chapter, this phenomenon will be explained in more detail.

Unfortunately, in some countries unscrupulous people have discovered a market in forming a link between wealthy Westerners who are willing to make donations or volunteer to improve the lives of 'poor orphans', and parents who are willing to sacrifice themselves by giving up their children so that they will have more to eat, an education and a rosy future.[14] In this way children and families are exploited so that people running the childcare institution can get rich on foreign donations: the 'orphanage industry'. In the third chapter, I will discuss the orphanage-industry that is created this way in more detail. I have had the misfortune to visit children's homes like these as well and in that chapter, I will give you a glimpse of what I found there.

So, there is a definite danger in sponsoring children's homes because it causes them to attract more and more children.[15] Particularly children who should not be there at all. However, as I shall explain further in the fourth chapter, the good news is that while most people still think of children's homes as the most appropriate and efficient way of taking care of children, this is quite simply not true, there are better and more cost-effective ways. Not only is living in a children's home not good for a child, of all the possible solutions to the various problems that lead to the child ending up in a children's home, it also the most expensive and most complicated to manage.[16]

In the fourth chapter, solutions will be provided that do not only give better results and provide a better outlook for the children, but that are also far cheaper and more cost-effective.

A question I am often asked is: But surely not all children's homes are evil, how do you tell the good ones from the bad? Unfortunately, the only positive answer to that is that not all children's homes are run with evil intent. In some children's homes, the people who work there really, genuinely want the very best for the children and do what they can to make sure they get it. These people honestly believe that they are providing the best possible solution for the children. However, unfortunately, even with the best intentions and the hardest work, children's homes are unable to meet all of a child's essential basic needs–which will be explained in detail in the second chapter–the consequences of which are serious and permanent.[17] So, to avoid any confusion, I should explicitly state that yes, I really do mean that children's homes should not exist at all.[18]

The only–more or less acceptable–exceptions are:

- Homes that provide temporary care–of no more than a few weeks or months at the most–while organising a reunion of the child with her family, or another form of placement in a family situation.[19]
- Small Group homes, where children who genuinely have no possibility of living with their

own family or another family are cared for in very small groups that form a kind of artificial family.[20]

It is important to remember that being raised by your parent, growing up with your family and living in the community are things specifically mentioned in the UN declarations of Human Rights, Child Rights and Rights of Persons with Disabilities.[21]

I have to warn you that this book is not going to be an enjoyable read. I will not apologise for this, because I feel that there is no way around it. I hope you will agree with me when you have finished reading this book. I believe it is very necessary to educate the public on what is happening, to keep well-meaning donors from causing unintentional harm despite only trying to help. I also think it is important to provide an array of viable alternatives that *will* have a positive impact on the lives of those we want to help. The only way to effectively spread awareness of the negative effects of children's homes on the lives of children who live there and the consequences of donating to them is to describe the reality. This book will give information about those consequences, as well as about the reasons why donating money causes more children to end up in 'orphanages' and why parents feel they have no choice by to give up their children, and what can be done to prevent those situations from arising.

I promise that my reasons for writing this book

are not to produce maximum shock or outrage, though I know I will likely be accused of that. After publishing something I wrote years ago, I was asked whether I had chosen the photos on the cover to produce a maximum shock-effect. I had to smile when I read that question because, in fact, I had taken great care to choose photos out of my extensive collection with the objective *not* to cause too much shock. I could have answered then, as I would now: Believe me, I could have done a lot worse. These images barely scratch the surface of what I have seen and experienced. I am not trying to shock you. I am only trying to give you enough of a glimpse to help you understand the seriousness of the situation.

---

1 Georgette Mulheir, Mara Cavanagh (2016) *Orphanage Entrepreneurs: The Trafficking of Haiti's Invisible Children* Lumos Foundation p7; John Williamson, Aaron Greenberg (2010) *Families, Not Orphanages* Better Care Network p8

2 Ariel Carroll (2015) *Terms of Reference: Funding stream analysis of residential care* Elevate Children Funders Group p2; Corinna Csaky (2009) *Keeping Children out of Harmful Institutions. Why We Should Be Investing in Family Based Care* The Save The Children Fund, London p12; Ghazal Kheshavarzian, Georgette Mulheir, Corinna Csaky (2015). *In Our Lifetime. How Donors Can End the Institutionalisation of Children.* Lumos, London p15

3 Kevin Browne (2009), *The Risk of Harm to Young Children in Institutional Care.* The Save The Children Fund, London p13

4 Kevin Browne (2009), *The Risk of Harm to Young Children in Institutional Care.* The Save The Children Fund, London p2; Ariel Carroll (2015) *Terms of Reference: Funding stream analysis of residential care* Elevate Children Funders Group p2; Ghazal Kheshavarzian, Georgette Mulheir, Corinna Csaky (2015). *In Our Lifetime. How Donors Can End the Institutionalisation of Children.* Lumos, London p15; Unknown (2014) *Ending the Institutionalisation of Children Globally – The Time Is Now* Lumos Foundation p6

5 https://www.unicef.org/media/media_45279.html

6 Ariel Carroll (2015) *Terms of Reference: Funding stream analysis of residential care* Elevate Children Funders Group p2; Corinna Csaky (2009) *Keeping Children out of Harmful Institutions. Why We Should Be Investing in Family Based Care* The Save The Children Fund, London p12

7 Ghazal Kheshavarzian, Georgette Mulheir, Corinna Csaky (2015). *In Our Lifetime. How Donors Can End the Institutionalisation of Children.* Lumos, London p15; Unicef (2010) *At Home or in a Home? Formal care and adoption of children in Eastern Europe and Central Asia* Geneva, Switzerland p23

8 Ariel Carroll (2015) *Terms of Reference: Funding stream analysis of residential care* Elevate Children Funders Group p2; Ghazal Kheshavarzian, Georgette Mulheir, Corinna Csaky (2015). *In Our Lifetime. How Donors Can End the Institutionalisation of Children.* Lumos, London p15; Unicef (2006) *Alternative Care for Children without Primary Caregivers in Tsunami Affected Countries. Indonesia, Malaysia, Myanmar and*

Thailand UNICEF East Asia and Pacific Regional Office, Thailand p29; John Williamson, Aaron Greenberg (2010) *Families, Not Orphanages* Better Care Network p7-8

9 Corinna Csaky (2009) *Keeping Children out of Harmful Institutions. Why We Should Be Investing in Family Based Care* The Save The Children Fund, London p10, 14; Ghazal Kheshavarzian, Georgette Mulheir, Corinna Csaky (2015). *In Our Lifetime. How Donors Can End the Institutionalisation of Children.* Lumos, London p15; Georgette Mulheir, Mara Cavanagh (2016) *Orphanage Entrepreneurs: The Trafficking of Haiti's Invisible Children* Lumos Foundation p8; Unicef (2010) *At Home or in a Home? Formal care and adoption of children in Eastern Europe and Central Asia* Geneva, Switzerland p23;

10 Corinna Csaky (2009) *Keeping Children out of Harmful Institutions. Why We Should Be Investing in Family Based Care* The Save The Children Fund, London p10, 14; Ghazal Kheshavarzian, Georgette Mulheir, Corinna Csaky (2015). *In Our Lifetime. How Donors Can End the Institutionalisation of Children.* Lumos, London p15

11 Kevin Browne (2009), *The Risk of Harm to Young Children in Institutional Care.* The Save The Children Fund, London p7-8; Unknown (2014) Website: CRIN *DISABLED CHILDREN: The African Report on Children with Disabilities: Promising Starts and Persisting Challenges*

12 Corinna Csaky (2009) *Keeping Children out of Harmful Institutions. Why We Should Be Investing in Family Based Care* The Save The Children Fund, London p10; Unicef (2010) *At Home or in a Home? Formal care and adoption of children in Eastern Europe and Central Asia* Geneva, Switzerland p23

13 Eric Mathews, Eric Rosenthal, Laurie Ahern,

Halyna Kurylo (2015) *No Way Home: The exploitation and abuse of children in Ukraine's orphanages* Disability Rights International USA p28-29

14 Corinna Csaky (2009) *Keeping Children out of Harmful Institutions. Why We Should Be Investing in Family Based Care* The Save The Children Fund, London p14; Unknown (2014) *Orphanage Trafficking and Orphanage Voluntourism. Frequently asked questions.* Next Generation Nepal p4, 6

15 Eric Mathews, Eric Rosenthal, Laurie Ahern, Halyna Kurylo (2015) *No Way Home: The exploitation and abuse of children in Ukraine's orphanages* Disability Rights International USA p65

16 Ariel Carroll (2015) *Terms of Reference: Funding stream analysis of residential care* Elevate Children Funders Group p2; Ghazal Kheshavarzian, Georgette Mulheir, Corinna Csaky (2015). *In Our Lifetime. How Donors Can End the Institutionalisation of Children.* Lumos, London p17

17 Georgette Mulheir, Kevin Browne (2007) *De-Institutionalisation and Transforming Children's Services. A guide to good practise.* European Commission Daphne Programme, UK p30

18 Unknown (2014) *Orphanage Trafficking and Orphanage Voluntourism. Frequently asked questions.* Next Generation Nepal p7; Ghazal Kheshavarzian, Georgette Mulheir, Corinna Csaky (2015). *In Our Lifetime. How Donors Can End the Institutionalisation of Children.* Lumos, London

19 John Williamson, Aaron Greenberg (2010) *Families, Not Orphanages* Better Care Network p3-4

20 Corinna Csaky (2009) *Keeping Children out of Harmful Institutions. Why We Should Be Investing in Family Based Care* The Save The Children Fund, London p10, p23;

Unknown (2014) *Ending the Institutionalisation of Children Globally – The Time Is Now* Lumos Foundation p7

21 Unknown (1948) *Universal Declaration of Human Rights*; Unknown (1989) *United Nations Convention on the Rights of the Child*: Unknown (2006) *United Nations Convention on the Rights of Persons with Disabilities*

The Effects of Growing Up in a Children's Home

This chapter was adapted from Florence Koenderink (2012) Children Everywhere. How to Provide Good Institutional Care to Infants and Toddlers. Book 1: Essential Elements of Childcare in Institutions Orphanage Projects, UK, Part 1, Chapter 5.

For a long time, it was widely believed that children would do just as well, if not better, when they were raised in a children's home compared to being raised in a family.[1] The thought behind that was that trained caregivers were far more qualified to raise children than parents, who did not have any training in childcare. During the twentieth century, this belief started to change. Some of the original belief still persists to this day, however.[2] It is now widely accepted that children are better off growing up with their parents *if* they do not have a severe physical or intellectual handicap and have two living parents who are at least moderately wealthy, not part of a repressed minority, and able to provide them with an education. However, the belief still exists in many places that if a child is handicapped, if one or both parents are dead, if the parents are very poor, if the family belongs to an ethnicity or religion that is stigmatised in their community, or if the child does not have access to formal education, she will be better off in a children's home. With regards to religion, it is regularly thought that receiving a more thorough religious upbringing–particularly in the case of a minority religion–will give the child a better life.[3] Even in the West, to this day, putting a child into a children's home is often still thought of as not ideal, but better than the alternatives.[4] This is very unfortunate, because no matter how persistent these beliefs about the benefits of institutional childcare are, they are false. In this chapter, I will attempt to show you just how far the care in a children's home is removed from that in a family, as well as the profound effect of that difference on children.

Things like food, hygiene, shelter, sleep and safety are generally recognised as basic needs. These are universally acknowledged to be things children require to be able to survive and thrive. It is much rarer for people–anywhere in the world–to realise that affection, attention, physical contact, stimulation and attachment are needs that are just as basic and essential.[5] In this book, I will refer to the generally recognised basic needs as 'practical needs' (food, hygiene, shelter, sleep and safety) and to the complete set of basic needs as 'essential basic needs' (practical needs plus affection, attention, physical contact, stimulation and attachment). Few people realise that a child's survival can depend on these things. Researchers have found that in Europe and the USA before 1920, when the standard practice was to only feed children, keep them clean, and provide them with a roof over their heads, but not to take care of the other essential basic needs, between 70 to 100% of children in orphanages did not survive.[6]

Receiving affection, attention, stimulation, physical contact and opportunities to form secure attachments is part of our essential basic needs, from birth onward. Especially in children's homes, these needs are often forgotten or pushed way down the priority list as a luxury. They are not a luxury. Children who for a long time do not receive physical contact, stimulation, attention, and the opportunity to form secure attachments aside from having their practical needs met, become emotionally scarred and in some cases even intellectually handicapped–if they survive.[7] Let's take a moment to have a look at the contrast between care in a family and that in an institution, and weigh the consequences.

A child in a family is usually surrounded by love and affection. This is often not said in words, but it is clear from the way parents talk to their children, give them attention, touch them and look at them. In most families, there is quite a lot of physical contact, especially when children are small. Babies are held and carried around on a parent's arm or in a sling of some kind. Toddlers get to sit on a parent's lap and older children regularly get a hug, lean against their parents or hold their hand in the street to be guided.

The combination of these things makes a child feel safe.[8] She feels that she has someone looking out for her, protecting her. The natural love and pride that parents feel for their children is expressed without being consciously noticed.

Caregivers in a children's home do not have this natural bond with the children in their care; the love does not come automatically, and it is certainly not expressed without noticing. In a children's home, caregivers are doing a job. They are usually kept busy trying to meet the child's practical needs such as making her food, keeping her clean and washing her clothes. This leaves little time for holding children and giving them real attention. In a family, these things are done automatically, while in a children's home they are often simply forgotten.

Children show a physiological response to not having their essential basic needs met. One consequence is that their production of growth hormones decreases, meaning the child only grows very slowly, or may even stop growing and developing altogether.[9] Children growing up in children's homes are always considerably smaller than children of the same age who live in the same area with their family.[10]

Another physiological effect is that their immune system becomes less active–in babies, it can even stop working completely.[11] This means that children in children's homes are more prone to illnesses and infections. When they get ill, it is likely to be a lot more serious than it would be for a child with a properly functioning immune-system.[12] When the immune-system stops working completely, any virus or infection can kill a baby.[13]

Even what children are capable of feeling for the rest of their lives is affected by whether or not the child has a sense of security, which develops by having essential basic needs met at a young age.[14] Small babies are not able to comfort themselves. When a baby cries and someone does not come soon to calm and sooth her by holding her, rocking her and fixing whatever is not right, she will cry with more and more desperation. This is a stressful experience for her, and if it happens often, or if she is left to cry for very long periods of time, it can even be traumatic. The hormones produced during this kind of stress can cause permanent damage to the brain and other body systems.[15] To compensate for the constant onslaught of stress, the brain can either become numb and unresponsive to all emotions and events[16] or become hyper-sensitive and hyper-aroused.[17] In case of the latter response, a default position of almost constant stress and anxiety develops for life.

Not only a child's size and her health are influenced by whether she receives enough physical contact and stimulation; the development of her brain also strongly depends on whether these needs are met.[18] There is a measurable difference in brain size between children who live in families (and are exposed to regular physical contact and freedom to play) and children who grow up in a situation with many children to few caregivers (where physical contact and freedom to play and develop is extremely limited or absent). The brains of children in children's homes are shown to be 20 to 30% smaller than those of children in families.[19] We are talking about actual brain matter that has never developed.[20]

The reason for these differences in development is that stimulation of all kinds leads to the creation of synapses and pathways in the brain. Links between different parts of the brain that are needed for it to work properly, to be able to process and integrate information. If there is no stimulation, no new synapses or pathways are formed. Lack of stimulation not only prevents the making of new synapses and pathways, it also leads to the destruction of existing connections. Of the connections a child is born with, only those that are used are kept. Others are destroyed to prevent clutter in the brain and have everything work efficiently.[21] Young children need to have their essential basic needs met to be able to develop important synapses and pathways and to keep existing ones intact.[22] When a child reaches the age of ten, the phase of rapid early brain growth and the development of the main connections is completed, and it will stop. This means that what has not been created by then, or what has already been destroyed, is quite simply lost, creating gaps in the brain's foundation. So, if these things do not happen when the child is small, it is too late. The child will simply have to live without them. When that is the case, the foundation on which all further brain development will be built, will not be sturdy. Plus, experiences such as physical contact, having the opportunity to form attachments, and being talked to from a very early age all together determine how well the brain is prepared for future learning and how well the two halves of the brain coordinate and process information together. Without full cooperation between the two brain halves, learning and information processing will be a lot harder.[23]

In a family, a child has a primary caregiver, usually a parent. A bond is formed with the primary caregiver and the child learns that this is someone she can depend on. The same is true for other people who are always around or return regularly in a child's life: her father, her siblings, and maybe uncles or aunts or grandparents who live in the same home or nearby. These relationships, formed at a very young age–unnoticed–teach the child how to form a relationship with someone and how to maintain it. The parts of the brain needed to form and maintain relationships are developed and strengthened in the course of this early learning. These lessons are needed later in life. They are important for forming and maintaining future relationships of all kinds, including those with future children of their own.[24]

The ability to form attachments with people needs to be learned at a young age. Children who are not exposed to positive social behaviour when they are very young make few connections in the relevant brain area. Children who live in a family usually do not even notice that they are learning, because they simply pick up the information from having a role in a normal family situation, from receiving the love of their family members and from having their needs met. Nobody needs to explain to a child in a family what relationships are and how to form them. In fact, it is not even possible to do so. The child gets to experience different kinds of relationships and through them she learns how to form bonds with other people.[25] Children who do not get the chance to form a special bond with a primary caregiver, do not form the links in their brains to make this kind of thing happen automatically later in life.[26] This can make it difficult–for some children even impossible–to form any kind of normal relationship later in life.[27]

In a children's home, there are usually few adults taking care of many children. Plus, caregivers in children's homes quite often vary from day to day and from year to year.[28] This can be because a caregiver leaves her job and someone else takes over or because caregivers work in shifts and are only available at certain days and certain times. It can also be because the children's home is divided into different age groups, or only caters to children up to a certain age, requiring children to move from one group or home to another when they grow older.[29] Furthermore, even when caregivers do live at the children's home and are available around the clock, they often look after so many children that there is not enough time to allow for time with individual children to form bonds. All of this means that the child does not get the chance to learn how to form relationships because the opportunity for forming bonds is not there. Problems related to attachment are often seen in children who spent much of their childhood in a children's home.[30]

One of these problems is indiscriminate attachment behaviour. A child with indiscriminate attachment behaviour has such a great need for positive attention and affection that she will not care what risks are involved in going up to strangers. She will go up to anyone and be open, trusting and affectionate without making a difference between people she knows and strangers.[31] Children who live in a family and who have bonded with their parents from an early age have a resistance toward strangers starting at about nine months of age.[32] This mistrust of strangers is built into human beings to keep them safe, because initially, you have no way of knowing whether a stranger can be trusted or not. For a child with indiscriminate attachment behaviour, the need for attention and affection is so much greater than the need to stay safe, that this built-in safety mechanism is thrown aside.[33]

Visitors who come to a children's home often

think the way children flock towards them, grabbing their hands, trying to sit on their laps is wonderful. Most people see it as a sign that the children are open and welcoming. In fact, it is a sign of indiscriminate attachment behaviour: it is a problem.[34] Children who have had indiscriminate attachment behaviour for several years may continue to go to strangers even after they are placed in a permanent adoptive family.[35] Even though they now have a secure home with a primary caregiver and lots of affection and attention, the need to find attention and affection wherever you can get it is imprinted in their brain to such an extent that they are just as likely to walk up to a stranger in a shop and take his hand, as they are to go to their adoptive mother.

Another problem related to attachment is resistance to bonding. A child who shows resistance to bonding has given up hope that someone will provide her with attention and affection. Rather than risk being disappointed and rejected again, she prefers to not even try to bond with other people and she rejects their efforts to bond with her. She is convinced that even if they try to interact or bond with her now, they will find out she is not worth it in the end and they will abandon her. So, instead of taking the risk of rejection, she withdraws within herself, making as little contact as possible with the outside world, to protect herself from any hurt she is sure will follow.[36]

Lack of dependable, primary caregivers in

a children's home can lead to the absence of a relationship between a child and the caregivers. However, it can also lead to such a great need to form an attachment that the child will even form a bond with someone who does not fulfil her essential basic needs. Children may sometimes even form an attachment to an abusive parent or caregiver.[37] Attachment does not have to come from both sides. It is possible for a child to attach herself to someone who does not respond to her attachment in the way she needs. However, an attachment to a caregiver who is abusive or who does not provide everything the child needs to stay healthy and develop properly is likely to be a disorganised attachment.[38] This means that while the child has attached to the caregiver and will try to stay near her whenever she can, she also knows that she cannot fully depend on the caregiver. The child may show conflicting behaviour, which can include sudden aggression or withdrawal. This behaviour and the inability to form proper, stable relationships can continue into adult life.

Vorria et al. did a study on attachment of 100 children aged between five days and five years old in a children's home in Greece. [39] The daily schedule of this home has the children in their beds 17.5 hours a day. They play outside of their beds for 3.5 hours a day and the remaining 3 hours accounts for the time it takes to feed and change them. While an earlier study of these same children showed that most children did develop some attachment, the quality of attachment had not been looked at. In the current study, it was found that 66% of the children formed disorganised attachments–an indication for later behavioural problems–compared to 25% of the children from the comparison group of children with two-parent-families. This is a similar result as is found for children of mothers who were depressed, alcoholic, mentally ill or who maltreated their children.

The lack of opportunity to form a secure attachment to a primary caregiver in the first three years of life also has serious psychological and behavioural effects, not only in the case of disorganised attachment. In the course of bonding with a primary caregiver, a child learns things like empathy and self-control.[40] Experiencing a close personal relationship is the only way she can learn about this. She learns to control her own behaviour and, to understand that other people have feelings and how they can be affected through constant interaction with a trusted primary caregiver, who helps her make sense of and control her emotions and who explains about other people's feelings.[41] Without empathy, a child cannot develop a conscience at a later age, and in extreme cases she might not even really see other people as people.[42] If she does not develop 'theory of mind', she may not realise that she needs to take other people's feelings and well-being into account, because she does not understand that they *have* feelings and thoughts of their own. In extreme cases, she may only see people as instruments to get what she wants.

Without developing empathy and self-control she is very likely to become impulsive, anxious and even aggressive or violent when she is older. This can make her a very dangerous person when she grows up–even psychopathic, in extreme cases.[43]

Young children are still trying to understand the meaning of all the things they see, hear, smell and feel around them. They need adults with whom they feel safe and whom they trust to help them interpret the meaning of all these things. This kind of information is constantly given to children who live in a family, throughout daily life. Most of the time, parents are unaware that they are helping their child make sense of the world. They are just reacting to situations the way they always do, and the baby observes this. By observing her parents' reactions, the child learns–through imitation–what things she should fear, what should be respected, what should be appreciated, what should be disdained, and so on.[44] In a children's home, this kind of information is usually lacking, because caregivers spend less time around the child than parents do and they often do not interact with the children very much. If a child does not receive information about how the world works, it can leave a great, deep confusion. Not learning about things being harmless, about difficult situations resolving themselves or about help to get through a difficult situation can deprive a child of the opportunity to learn to calm and soothe herself.

In a similar way, children depend on their parents–or a trusted caregiver with whom they have bonded–to help them develop a sense of self.[45] In a family, the way parents act towards a child and the way they introduce her to and guide her through the world gives the child a sense of identity, self-respect, and self-confidence, as well as a feeling of belonging, culture and status.[46] In a children's home, it is much more difficult to provide a child with these things, because a children's home is usually a world of its own, cut off from the outside world.[47] This means that children do not learn how to behave in everyday social situations such as buying things in a shop, meeting people in the street or having family members over for a visit. They do not get the information they need to build up their identity.[48] Children in families pick up how to behave without noticing by watching adults handle these situations every day.

It is not uncommon for children in children's homes–especially if they are part of a minority of some sort–to be completely unaware of their background and their ethnic, cultural and/or religious identity. Sometimes this is because the people running the children's home wish to raise the children within a 'superior', majority culture, thinking that the children will be better off staying away from their heritage. Or, in countries where there are a lot of tensions between different tribes or ethnic backgrounds, the aim is to reach equality and brotherhood through erasing and denying individual identities, usually with the best intentions. Either way, it is not fair on the children to keep them away from their cultural heritage. It is an essential part of their identity, and they should have the opportunity to learn about it.[49]

A children's home is usually run in a way that makes life easier for the caregivers. This is understandable, because a children's home is often set up more like a business than like a home. In business, best practice is to make things easier on the staff–the caregivers. Mealtimes and other activities are planned at times that work well for the caregivers. When caregivers are all busy attending to practical things, children are expected to stay quiet and out of the way. In some places, they are simply put in their beds or locked in a room, with nothing to do. The business model does not take into account that the 'goods' handled in this particular business are not objects, but human beings. Children.[50]

In some institutional situations where staff-to-child ratios are very low, and stimulation, attention and personal connections are rare to non-existent, children may withdraw into themselves, trying to deny the things that are lacking in their living situation.[51] By using stereotypical behaviour such as rocking or banging their heads, and sometimes pulling out their own hair, children try to provide themselves with some kind of stimulation where all other is lacking. At the same time, they try to shut out the outside world.[52] In some cases, this can even turn into institutional autism, a form of autism that starts in a child who used to be normal, because of a long-term severe lack of having essential basic needs met.[53]

I regularly get complaints–from people working in children's homes all over the world–about children who have lived in a home with many children and few caregivers for several years. These complaints are always very similar: I am told that the children are badly-behaved, ill-mannered, disobedient, disrespectful, rebellious and ungrateful. It is made to sound like these are somehow exceptional children, very bad ones. They ask me how they can make the children behave better. It always saddens me to hear this because the behaviour seen in these children is the natural and inevitable result of being raised without getting attention, affection, a chance to form attachments, proper stimulation or positive role models.[54] There is nothing inherently wrong or bad about these children. Any child put in that position would either turn out the same way, or not survive. As for being ungrateful, these children did not ask to be put in a place where their essential basic needs are not met, and it is easy to see how they do not feel they have much to be grateful for, no matter how good the intentions of the people running the children's home are.

Another problem is that when you burden a caregiver with too many children–in some cases, this can be more than 20 children, even babies, to one caregiver–to allow her to provide proper care that meets the essential basic needs, something happens in the mind of the caregiver. Being overwhelmed with too many children, who are not doing well due to lack of proper care, the caregiver will feel forced to 'take a step back' in her mind. If she gets too close to the children and too involved with them, the fact that these children are wilting away under her care becomes too much of a psychological burden. So out of self-preservation and to be able to keep the job, which she needs to feed her own family, she starts dehumanizing the children.[55] This is not a conscious decision, it is something that simply happens. By not seeing the children as human beings anymore, she does not need to worry too much about whether they are happy and healthy and she is able to get on with the practical aspects of her job. This behaviour is very understandable and you can hardly blame her for it. The unfortunate thing is that once a caregiver does not see the children as human beings anymore, she is no longer motivated to put effort into making sure the children are well. All she will feel she needs to do, is enough to keep her job. In this situation both neglect and abuse can, and do, easily get out of hand.[56] In other words, the care the children receive will get worse and worse.[57]

Once a child is moved from a children's home into a family, either through adoption or fostering, some of the problems that have been mentioned may partly be solved. Usually, this requires a lot of therapy, hard work and patience on the part of the new parents.[58] However, some of the damage done is permanent and cannot be fixed, because it is quite simply part of the way the child's brain has developed.[59] This is especially true if the child was put in a children's home before she was three years old and if she was there for several years.[60]

I would like to share the story of an experience I had with a little girl, which will illustrate many of the things mentioned in this chapter.

> When I arrived at the children's home, I found one dorm where 16 children aged one to six years old were cared for by one caregiver. The vegetarian diet given to the children was not well-balanced, so all of the children showed various degrees of malnutrition. One child was much worse off than the others. She was a little girl of eighteen months old, she weighed 4.5kg and her height was 63cm. Her arms, legs and buttocks had lost all muscles and her belly was terribly bloated. She sat quietly on the floor, not really moving. Occasionally, she made a hand gesture to indicate that she wanted to eat or drink, but usually no one noticed and if they did not, she gave up immediately. She had fallen into a vicious cycle. The caregiver was extremely busy trying to take care of all 16 children as well as possible, and she had her hands full dealing with the various demands they made. The little girl got weakened by a diet that was not quite balanced, but not terrible. Getting weaker, she needed more care, but was too weak to demand it and the caregiver was

only able to go from one demand to the next, which caused the little girl to weaken further, making it even less likely that she would find the energy to fight for her needs. And so it continued, until the present stage was reached: severe malnutrition, serious dehydration and bronchitis, all on top of being HIV-positive.

The little girl was so severely malnourished and dehydrated that when I found her, there was no guarantee that she would survive. She needed medical help and food and drink, but more than anything she needed physical contact, attention and affection. For her to have any chance of survival, she needed to have the undivided attention of a caregiver, to be held constantly and to be offered food and drink every hour, if not more often. With all caregivers in this home looking after 15 to 20 children each, this seemed impossible. However, in the home there was also a fourteen-year-old girl who refused to attend school. She had expressed an interest in childcare, and already acted as a caregiver's assistant. Based on how she dealt with small children, she clearly had quite a lot of insight into what they needed, as well as a lot of love for the children. So, it was decided to ask her if she would be willing to take on the little malnourished girl's care, under supervision. She agreed and got to work straightaway, with incredible dedication.

Effectively, the teenager became the little girl's foster mother, and she showed all the protectiveness and possessiveness of a real mother. Changes were also made to the diet of the small children, which brought some improvement, although it was still not an altogether balanced diet. Yet the little girl started gaining weight, growing, and catching up on her developmental milestones within a few weeks' time. The little girl's need for physical contact, attention and affection turned out to be even more urgent than her need for the right food.

It was more than two years before I was able to visit the same project again and none of the younger children really remembered me anymore. When I arrived at the dorm where the little girl stayed, all 18 other children (more had been added to the group in the time I had been away) came out of the room to hug me and hold my hands and try to sit on my lap, even though they did not know who I was anymore. The little girl followed after them much more slowly and kept watching me from a distance. Because she had had a chance to attach to her 'foster mother', her healthy fear of strangers was not thrown overboard, and she made sure I could be trusted before approaching me, much later.

This little girl is now seven years old and attending school. She is doing well and is pretty healthy, but she will always stay very small because of her early deprivation. At first sight, most people will guess she is a three or four-year-old now.

Research has shown again and again that even if a child gets an education in a children's home, one which she might not have gotten with her family, she is unlikely to be successful in her adult life and runs a very high risk of ending up living in the streets.[61] This is particularly unfortunate because many children's homes are opened especially to keep children off the streets. It has been shown that even if the child lives in severe poverty with her family, and receives little or no education, her chances in life are better than those of a child who was raised in a children's home. The main reason for this is most likely that her essential basic needs were met by her family, giving her body and her brain a better chance of developing normally, which almost never happens in a children's home.

A study of young adults who had grown up in children's homes found that they were

- 10 times more likely to be involved in prostitution as adults
- 40 times more likely to have a criminal record
- 500 times more likely to commit suicide[62]

Understanding the big difference between the care children receive in a family and the care they get in a children's home, and the terrible consequences of that difference, should make it easier to understand why children should never be placed in a children's home. Even in the best children's homes, there is still a gap compared to care in a family: essential basic needs are never fully met.[63] In the next chapter I will show that this is the case even in places with a good caregiver-to-child ratio. Hopefully getting a little bit of insight into this, has convinced you that 'orphanages' or children's home are not the best investment to make if you want to help vulnerable children.

1 Kevin Browne (2009), *The Risk of Harm to Young Children in Institutional Care.* The Save The Children Fund, London p3

2 Georgette Mulheir, Mara Cavanagh (2016) *Orphanage Entrepreneurs: The Trafficking of Haiti's Invisible Children* Lumos Foundation p7-8; Maia Szalavitz (2010) How Orphanages Kill Babies -- And Why No Child Under 5 Should Be In One. *Huffington Post, 23 April 2010*

3 Bjarte Sanne (2008) *Understanding the Child. A mental needs manual for caretakers in children's homes 2nd Edition* p42

4 Corinna Csaky (2009) *Keeping Children out of Harmful Institutions. Why We Should Be Investing in Family Based Care* The Save The Children Fund, London p13

5 Bjarte Sanne (2008) *Understanding the Child. A mental needs manual for caretakers in children's homes 2nd Edition*; John Williamson, Aaron Greenberg (2010) *Families, Not Orphanages* Better Care Network p5

6 Bjarte Sanne (2008) *Understanding the Child. A mental needs manual for caretakers in children's homes 2nd Edition* p41-42; John Williamson, Aaron Greenberg (2010) *Families, Not Orphanages* Better Care Network p10

7 Georgette Mulheir, Mara Cavanagh (2016) *Orphanage Entrepreneurs: The Trafficking of Haiti's Invisible Children* Lumos Foundation p8; John Williamson, Aaron Greenberg (2010) *Families, Not Orphanages* Better Care Network p5-6; Unknown (2014) *Ending the Institutionalisation of Children Globally – The Time Is Now* Lumos Foundation p3

8 Terry M. Levy, Michael Orlans (2000), *Attachment Disorders as an Antecedent to Violence and Antisocial Patterns in Children* p4; Georgette Mulheir, Kevin Browne (2007) *De-Institutionalisation and Transforming Children's Services. A guide to good practise.* European Commission Daphne Programme, UK p29

9 Ariel Carroll (2015) *Terms of Reference: Funding stream analysis of residential care* Elevate Children Funders Group p1; Bjarte Sanne (2008) *Understanding the Child. A mental needs manual for caretakers in children's homes 2nd Edition* p239; Maia Szalavitz (2010) How Orphanages Kill Babies -- And Why No Child Under 5 Should Be In One. *Huffington Post, 23 April 2010*

10 Kevin Browne (2009), *The Risk of Harm to Young Children in Institutional Care.* The Save The Children Fund, London p10; Corinna Csaky (2009) *Keeping Children out of Harmful Institutions. Why We Should Be Investing in Family Based Care* The Save The Children Fund, London p15; Maia Szalavitz (2010) How Orphanages Kill Babies -- And Why No Child Under 5 Should Be In One. *Huffington Post, 23 April 2010*

11 Ibid.

12 Kevin Browne (2009), *The Risk of Harm to Young Children in Institutional Care.* The Save The Children Fund, London p10; Bjarte Sanne (2008) *Understanding the Child. A mental needs manual for caretakers in children's homes 2nd Edition* p238

13 Ariel Carroll (2015) *Terms of Reference: Funding stream analysis of residential care* Elevate Children Funders Group p1

14 Georgette Mulheir, Kevin Browne (2007) *De-*

Institutionalisation and Transforming Children's Services. A guide to good practise. European Commission Daphne Programme, UK p30

15 Maia Szalavitz (2010) How Orphanages Kill Babies -- And Why No Child Under 5 Should Be In One. *Huffington Post, 23 April 2010*

16 Georgette Mulheir, Kevin Browne (2007) *De-Institutionalisation and Transforming Children's Services. A guide to good practise.* European Commission Daphne Programme, UK p29

17 Terry M. Levy, Michael Orlans (2000), *Attachment Disorders as an Antecedent to Violence and Antisocial Patterns in Children* p8

18 Corinna Csaky (2009) *Keeping Children out of Harmful Institutions. Why We Should Be Investing in Family Based Care* The Save The Children Fund, London p15; Ghazal Kheshavarzian, Georgette Mulheir, Corinna Csaky (2015). *In Our Lifetime. How Donors Can End the Institutionalisation of Children.* Lumos, London p15

19 Ariel Carroll (2015) *Terms of Reference: Funding stream analysis of residential care* Elevate Children Funders Group p1

20 Maia Szalavitz (2010) How Orphanages Kill Babies -- And Why No Child Under 5 Should Be In One. *Huffington Post, 23 April 2010*

21 Bjarte Sanne (2008) *Understanding the Child. A mental needs manual for caretakers in children's homes 2nd Edition* p236-237

22 Kevin Browne (2009), *The Risk of Harm to Young Children in Institutional Care.* The Save The Children Fund, London p14-15

23 Georgette Mulheir, Kevin Browne (2007) *De-Institutionalisation and Transforming Children's Services. A guide to good practise.* European Commission Daphne Programme, UK p30; John Williamson, Aaron Greenberg (2010) *Families, Not Orphanages* Better Care Network p6; Kevin Browne (2009), *The Risk of Harm to Young Children in Institutional Care.* The Save The Children Fund, London p10

24 Kevin Browne (2009), *The Risk of Harm to Young Children in Institutional Care.* The Save The Children Fund, London p16-17

25 Terry M. Levy, Michael Orlans (2000), *Attachment Disorders as an Antecedent to Violence and Antisocial Patterns in Children* p4

26 Oliver Holmes (2016) *The Guardian:* 'Orphanage Tourism': fears of child exploitation boom as Myanmar opens up 29/09/2016

27 Ariel Carroll (2015) *Terms of Reference: Funding stream analysis of residential care* Elevate Children Funders Group p1-2

28 John Williamson, Aaron Greenberg (2010) *Families, Not Orphanages* Better Care Network p5-6

29 Unicef (2006) *Alternative Care for Children without Primary Caregivers in Tsunami Affected Countries. Indonesia, Malaysia, Myanmar and Thailand* UNICEF East Asia and Pacific Regional Office, Thailand p30

30 Kevin Browne (2009), *The Risk of Harm to Young Children in Institutional Care.* The Save The Children Fund, London p13

31 Ibid. p12; Bjarte Sanne (2008) *Understanding the Child. A mental needs manual for caretakers in children's homes 2nd Edition*

p198-199

32 Ibid. p8

33 John Williamson, Aaron Greenberg (2010) *Families, Not Orphanages* Better Care Network p6

34 Ibid. p6

35 Kevin Browne (2009), *The Risk of Harm to Young Children in Institutional Care.* The Save The Children Fund, London p16

36 Ibid p12; Bjarte Sanne (2008) *Understanding the Child. A mental needs manual for caretakers in children's homes 2nd Edition* p199

37 Marinus H. van IJzendoorn, Marian J. Bakermans-Kranenburg (2003) Attachment Disorders and Disorganised Attachment: Similar and Different. *Attachment and Human Development Vol 5 No 3 (September 2003)* p2

38 Kevin Browne (2009), *The Risk of Harm to Young Children in Institutional Care.* The Save The Children Fund, London p12-13

39 Panayiota Vorria et al (2003). Early Experiences and Attachment Relationships of Greek Infants Raised in Residential Group Care. *Journal of Child Psychology and Psychiatry* 44:0 (2003), pp 1-13 2

40 Corinna Csaky (2009) *Keeping Children out of Harmful Institutions. Why We Should Be Investing in Family Based Care* The Save The Children Fund, London p18; Maia Szalavitz, How Orphanages Kill Babies -- And Why No Child Under 5 Should Be In One. *Huffington Post, 23 April 2010*

41 Terry M. Levy, Michael Orlans (2000), *Attachment Disorders as an Antecedent to Violence and Antisocial Patterns in Children* p4-5

42 Georgette Mulheir, Kevin Browne (2007) *De-Institutionalisation and Transforming Children's Services. A guide to good practise.* European Commission Daphne Programme, UK p30

43 Terry M. Levy, Michael Orlans (2000), *Attachment Disorders as an Antecedent to Violence and Antisocial Patterns in Children* p2, 5-7

44 Bjarte Sanne (2008) *Understanding the Child. A mental needs manual for caretakers in children's homes 2nd Edition* p14

45 Ibid. p58-59

46 Terry M. Levy, Michael Orlans (2000), *Attachment Disorders as an Antecedent to Violence and Antisocial Patterns in Children* p4-5

47 Kevin Browne (2009), *The Risk of Harm to Young Children in Institutional Care.* The Save The Children Fund, London p9

48 Corinna Csaky (2009) *Keeping Children out of Harmful Institutions. Why We Should Be Investing in Family Based Care* The Save The Children Fund, London p18

49 Bjarte Sanne (2008) *Understanding the Child. A mental needs manual for caretakers in children's homes 2nd Edition* p47

50 Kevin Browne (2009), *The Risk of Harm to Young Children in Institutional Care.* The Save The Children Fund, London p9

51 Georgette Mulheir, Kevin Browne (2007) *De-Institutionalisation and Transforming Children's Services. A guide to good practise.* European Commission Daphne Programme, UK p29

52 Kevin Browne (2009), *The Risk of Harm to Young Children in Institutional Care.* The Save The Children Fund, London p9, p10

53 Ibid. p12, 16; Dr. Ronald S. Federici (1998) *Help for the Hopeless Child: A Guide for Families*; Georgette Mulheir, Kevin Browne (2007) *De-Institutionalisation and Transforming Children's Services. A guide to good practise.* European Commission Daphne Programme, UK p30-31; Bjarte Sanne (2008) *Understanding the Child. A mental needs manual for caretakers in children's homes 2nd Edition* p198-200

54 Corinna Csaky (2009) *Keeping Children out of Harmful Institutions. Why We Should Be Investing in Family Based Care* The Save The Children Fund, London p15; Terry M. Levy, Michael Orlans (2000), *Attachment Disorders as an Antecedent to Violence and Antisocial Patterns in Children* p6

55 Craig Haney, Curtis Banks, Philip Zimbardo (1973) Interpersonal Dynamics in a Simulated Prison *International Journal of Criminology and Penology 1973, 1, 69-97* California, USA

56 Corinna Csaky (2009) *Keeping Children out of Harmful Institutions. Why We Should Be Investing in Family Based Care* The Save The Children Fund, London p16; Georgette Mulheir, Kevin Browne (2007) *De-Institutionalisation and Transforming Children's Services. A guide to good practise.* European Commission Daphne Programme, UK p31-33; Unknown (2015) Website: CRIN *Mexico: Authorities Fail to Protect Children & Adults with Disabilities from Torture, Trafficking & Segregation*

57 Eric Mathews, Eric Rosenthal, Laurie Ahern, Halyna Kurylo (2015) *No Way Home: The exploitation and abuse of children in Ukraine's orphanages* Disability Rights International USA p35

58 John Williamson, Aaron Greenberg (2010) *Families, Not Orphanages* Better Care Network p6

59 Kevin Browne (2009), *The Risk of Harm to Young Children in Institutional Care.* The Save The Children Fund, London p16

60 Terry M. Levy, Michael Orlans (2000), *Attachment Disorders as an Antecedent to Violence and Antisocial Patterns in Children* p9-11

61 Oliver Holmes (2016) *The Guardian:* 'Orphanage Tourism': fears of child exploitation boom as Myanmar opens up 29/09/2016; Unknown (2014) *Orphanage Trafficking and Orphanage Voluntourism. Frequently asked questions.* Next Generation Nepal p5

62 Unknown (2014) *Ending the Institutionalisation of Children Globally – The Time Is Now* Lumos Foundation p3; Corinna Csaky (2009) *Keeping Children out of Harmful Institutions. Why We Should Be Investing in Family Based Care* The Save The Children Fund, London p18-19

63 Ghazal Kheshavarzian, Georgette Mulheir, Corinna Csaky (2015). *In Our Lifetime. How Donors Can End the Institutionalisation of Children.* Lumos, London

What Is the Result of Donating?

We have seen that care in children's homes is not as good as care in a family, and that the consequences of living in a children's home can be very serious and permanent. Surely that means that we need to put *more* money into children's homes? Surely it means that we need to make sure that they are able to hire more caregivers, provide better food and get more training? On the face of it, it may look that way, but it is not the truth of the situation. However well a children's home is run, and however many caregivers are hired to take care of the children, a children's home will never be able to fulfil all of a child's essential basic needs.[1]

I have seen places where very good attempts were made, with only two to three children per caregiver and quite a lot of attention and stimulation within a large group setup. The results were certainly a lot better than in most other places, but they still did not come close to the way children's needs are met in families. There was still no proper opportunity for attachment, which means that the sense of security– which is crucial for proper development– was lacking. All children were small for their age, despite good quality food. And children did not get to observe and experience 'real life', they still lived in a cut-off world within the institution, meaning they did not get the opportunity to learn the everyday things all children need to learn to prepare them for adult life out in the real world.[2] I was able to stay in touch with some of the children who were adopted from this place over the years, and most of them showed various attachments disorders, behavioural problems and mental health issues, even after starting their life in stable family situations. Institutional care is not a good option.

There are many unfortunate side-effects to funding children's homes and I will discuss a range of them. I will start with some slightly less poignant truths about the effects of donating to children's homes, before we go on to the ugly core of the problem.

One of these 'lesser' disadvantages, is creating a dependency. While donations are made with the best of intentions, they sometimes have the effect of making the people who run the children's home feel not only indebted, but also dependent on their major donors. This is understandable and unavoidable to a certain extent: if they need your money to be able to feed their children and to pay their staff, they depend on you. But it can go further than that. I have seen cases where the people running the children's home essentially renounced all responsibility. They feel that it is up to you–the wealthy foreign donor–to make sure things are working well. After all, that is what you are there for, and from their perspective you have money to burn. So why should they put in time and effort to do things themselves? This is a very dangerous attitude, which can be very harmful for the children.

Opening a children's home means taking on a tremendous responsibility. Taking in children means accepting the burden of responsibility for their safety and well-being. Not just today and tomorrow, but for as long as they are living at the children's home. And it does not stop there, it continues with the children who come after them. This is something people who start a children's home should put some thought into, but often they do not. It is not just about making sure there is a roof over the children's head and a place for them to sleep, as a lot of people seem to think. Many people take the responsibility of running their home seriously, but not everyone is aware of how far the responsibility they have taken upon themselves stretches out, or how hard it is to live up to the implied promise to the children. 'God will provide' is something I have heard many times. It is a beautiful sentiment and it is admirable to put one's trust in God and to pray for what is needed. However, when there are several dozen hungry mouths to feed, you do not take your responsibility seriously if *all* you do is pray and wait for God to deliver what is needed. Some effort on the part of the person running the children's home is needed as well, to help God to provide.

A children's home manager told me about a former volunteer who still made regular donations to cover children's school fees, who had written an email to the children's home. In it, she mentioned that she had heard that the diet and hygiene standards at the home still left a lot to be desired–which was quite true. She wrote that she was disappointed. The manager of the home was very angry about the email. She told me: 'In December we had no money, NOTHING to feed the children. And *did* she send more money for food when we needed it?! Then how can she complain?' This manager had lost any feeling of responsibility for making sure the children had something to eat. While she usually phrased it as 'God will provide,' what she meant was: 'The donors and volunteers had better come and solve this quickly: look at the state of the children!'

Another problem is that it seems some people think that bigger is better. In the case of children's homes, this is certainly never true when it comes to the well-being of the children. In fact, the smaller the children's home, the greater the chances that essential basic needs are met, at least to some extent. There are people who want their children's home to be as big as possible, not so much because they think it will be better for the children, but because it will give them a better reputation. They hope to be seen as even more noble, self-sacrificing and wonderful if they 'take care' of more children, and maybe donors will be willing to pay up when they see the great number of children in need. While it may be true that some people admire this kind of attitude, I am sure I am not the only one who frowns upon it instead.

Anyone who knows what is involved in taking proper care of children knows that in children's homes where more than 50 children are cared for, children generally only have their practical needs met, if those. Why the threshold is at that number is not clear to me, but I have noticed repeatedly over the past ten years that children's home with more than 50 children never come close to providing the care needed by the children, while homes with fewer than 50 children sometimes meet at least a few of the psychological needs as well as the practical ones.[3] In institutional childcare, the bigger-is-better-rule seems to work exactly the other way around: the smaller the home, the better the chance of reasonably good care. While 50 children is a limit above which you are guaranteed to move into terrible care, keeping below 12 children–in total–is the only way to have a decent chance of being able to provide good care.[4]

When I see a brochure of a children's home currently caring for 50 children–and struggling to provide them with food–saying that they aim to care for 300 children within five years, it does not make me admire them. It makes me wonder if they care for the children in their home at all. That kind of expansion can only happen at the cost of the children in the home. More likely than not it will not only lead to even less attention, supervision and stimulation, but also to more overcrowding, poorer hygiene and more malnutrition.

I regularly get emails asking me to send money to orphanages, to help them out. The emails are designed to make people start crying and pull out their wallet. However, when I received an email–not at all an exception–that says that the home cared for 60 children and those children regularly went to bed hungry, it did not make me want to pull out my wallet. It made me want to scream at the computer: '*Why* did you take in 60 children, if you don't know how to feed them!'[5]

However, unfortunately, well-meaning people trying to do their very best to give children who have nowhere else to go better lives and finding out that their best is not good enough to give the children what they need are not the greatest problem. Nor are people who take in too many children, or people who do not take their responsibility towards the children seriously enough. We have arrived at the gruelling part of the unintended side-effects of donating to children's homes.

Even when you have read articles in newspapers or maybe seen a documentary about the 'orphanage industry',[6] it is still hard to wrap your head around. I experienced that myself. Even though I had heard of so-called orphanages recruiting children who have families in order to get donations from foreigners, the reality of the situation did not really hit home until I witnessed several examples of children's homes that existed for no other reason than to make money for their founders. I would like to share a story of my first real-life experience of the orphanage industry with you.

Someone contacted me through my website, saying that he was planning to start a children's home and he wanted my help.

> As usual, I started out by explaining that I would not provide any money, but that I would be happy to help him in other ways, if I could. He wrote back that he would be happy with any kind of help. Although he did not have a children's home yet, he contacted me quite regularly. He was also very insistent that I come to visit, to meet him and see how I could help. I found this a little strange, because there was no children's home yet and no staff had been recruited that I could help train. However, in the end I agreed to make a two-week visit to his area, to find out what was going on and whether it was worth getting involved by establishing an ongoing project.
>
> When I got to the country and we met, the man–whom I will call J.–immediately took me to see his cousin with whom he lives and who runs an 'orphanage' with 12 children. J. and his cousin spent a lot of time giving me an honoured welcome and explaining the situation. The cousin told me about the poor and remote conditions of the village from which he came, and from which he had brought the children to the big city to make sure they would have an education and healthcare. He emphasised how backward everything was in the village: there was no electricity, there were no schools or health centres, and

no opportunities for the children. He explained, in detail, how he was sacrificing his life and career opportunities to make sure that these children would have an education.

Over the next several days, I was taken to visit three other 'orphanages', run by J's friends and family members. Each of them cared for 6 to 18 children, ranging in age from six to sixteen years old. There was no caregiving staff, the children just lived in a house with the founder, who in some cases had a wife and children or parents living in the same house. The homes had been running anywhere between two and eight years at that point. Despite the beautiful stories of sacrifice and giving the children a better life, the reality was that the school-age children lived in a house in the city with the person who set up the 'orphanage'. They were removed from the family, the village and the life they knew, and taken to the completely different life of the city. They received food, clothes, schooling and tuition and when they were not in school they were expected to behave well and take care of chores like cleaning, cooking and generally serving the founder and his guests. Attention, affection, and concern for the children's emotional well-being were rarely seen. For the most part, the children's presence was simply tolerated, like that of the furniture. If a child does not do well in school, it is blamed on laziness or badness.

In an attempt to impress me, the cousin said that he wanted to give the children an opportunity to learn and develop a creative mind. So, he gave them money and allowed them to buy whatever they wanted with it at the market and to cook it how they wanted. He would eat whatever came out of that, together with the children, without complaining. This sounded admirable, on the surface. However, the reality was that the fourteen-year-old girl spent all of the time she was not in school in the kitchen, cooking three meals a day for 16 people. She only came out of the kitchen when she needed to serve the adults, or was ordered to do more chores.

When I asked whether these children ever got to visit their families, the answer was 'no' in all cases. When I asked whether these children were in contact with their family at all, the answer was only 'yes' in some cases. I was told that it was too difficult, because of the great distance, the great cost and the difficulty of reaching the remote villages that these children came from. I was also told that if they were allowed to visit their family, they might not want to come back again. That as long as they were in school, they would live in the children's homes, and when they would finish their studies–in four, eight, or twelve years' time–they would be free to go back if they wished. But after so much time without any contact with their family, having lived in a city and not being used to rural life anymore, what will they feel they have to go back to?

I was asked to speak to the children in each of the children's homes I visited. I was made to sit on a chair, while the children sat on the floor at my feet and essentially I was requested to tell the children–as a higher authority–to be better behaved and to work harder at school. Instead, I spoke to them about how sometimes it can be difficult to believe that you are worth something, but that they really all were very important. And that it is important to keep dreaming and trying to work towards that dream, even when it seems there is no point. With the little room I was given, I was trying to make the children feel that they were someone, that they mattered. In the homes that had been running for less than four years, I was able to reach individual children. By making eye-contact and smiling at them, and by directing parts of what I was saying at individual children, I was able to bring down their guards and draw out the child inside, just for a moment. A twinkle would return to little eyes and sometimes a smile would appear. In the home that had been going for eight years, I was unable to reach anyone. The children had withdrawn so far within themselves–out of self-preservation–that I was unable to reach them in the limited time I had. These children were crushed and it was heart-breaking to witness.

It quickly became clear that these people were not in any way interested in information about how they could improve the quality of life for the children. They were simply looking for money and they were hoping that getting me to see things in person and telling me the stories of their hardship directly, they would be able to persuade me to pay up.

When the last few days of my stay in the country came around, I had given up on trying to get through to them on improving things for the children, as it was clear that it would not work anyway. They, on the other hand, with a certain sense of desperation, cranked up their efforts to get money out of me–without ever asking for money directly–by bringing out even worse stories of hardship, suffering, and sacrifice, designed to get me to weep my way to my wallet. I only nodded and smiled and agreed that it was really terrible, while thinking that the real horror was those blank-faced children spread around the room. They seemed to have the impression that I must be really thick not to get the message. I was also regularly asked if I had any Christian friends who might want to visit or donate to the 'orphanage'.

Just before I left, I happened to see an announcement that UNICEF was planning to open schools and clinics in the remote area that J. and his cousin had told me they were from. So, when I visited them again, I mentioned this news and asked them if that was not wonderful, that the children would be able to get education and healthcare while staying with their own family. Their first reaction was that that was probably not in the same region, because that region was so backwards that it did not generally receive help. I mentioned that UNICEF usually goes to exactly those kinds of regions, to make sure that the most vulnerable children are reached first. They did not say anything to that, but it did not look like they thought it was wonderful news at all. After I left, J. still contacted me from time to time, but I have not given him much of a reaction.

It took me a while to figure out why J. suddenly decided that he wanted to open an 'orphanage' himself. He said that he felt it was his Christian duty to help these children. But he was living with his cousin, who was 'taking care' of 12 children already, so surely, he could help the children at his cousin's home? Then it struck me that J. was of an age to start thinking about marriage, which means he needed an income and a place to live. These are not easy things to get over there. But if you open an 'orphanage' and find a foreign donor to pay the rent, utilities and provide money for food, then you are set up. It is not a scheme that will make you rich, just to set yourself up without the bother of having to pay for basic necessities. And those children... ah well, they are around of course and that can be a nuisance, but on the whole, they keep pretty quiet and do not get in the way too much.

This is a depressing story, but it is important to remember that it is more than a story. It represents the lives these children lead.[7] Not only the children whom I met personally on this and other occasions, but many, many more. The phenomenon of the 'orphanage-industry', of people opening a children's home as a way of earning money through foreign donations and volunteer visits is not incidental or even rare. It is known to happen on a large scale in various countries in Asia, Africa and Latin-America.[8]

The reason people have come to see this as an opportunity is that in the last two or three decades, it has become popular among people in Western countries to make donations to 'orphanages', to sponsor a child 'without parents' or to volunteer in a children's home.[9] This exploits the children, their families, and the emotions that the concept of 'orphans' stirs up. While it does not always mean getting a lot of money out of foreigners' pockets–simply sharing in the housing and the food for the children, paid for by foreign donations and maybe inflating the monthly cost by a dollar or two provides a comfortable living in many places–it is still a form of exploitation. Some of these places may be run out of a sense of idealism: to give children an education or a better religious upbringing. However, there is still a clear motive of profit as well. And while money is prised out of the pockets of foreign donors, they are not the real victims here. Unwittingly, they are made into accomplices of the people running the 'orphanages'. The real victims are the children, who have been ripped away from their families and are often simply 'stored' in the 'orphanages', so that money can be made out of their presence. The children are the ones whose prospects in life deteriorate day by day.

Specific situations such as natural disasters have caused numerous 'orphanages', well-funded by generous foreigners, to pop up in recent years. Examples of this are the tsunami in Indonesia,[10] the earthquake in Nepal and the combination of the earthquake and the hurricane on Haiti.[11] Instead of starting organisations or teams that direct money towards reuniting children with their families, 'orphanages' were set up, without any real attempts to find the families the children belong to. Alternatively, families who have lost everything in these disasters and do not know how to feed their children or how to protect them from the cold are not offered help to take care of their children. Instead, they are told to give up their children to an 'orphanage' so that the child will be warm and fed. Parents are forced to make the sacrifice of giving up their children in an attempt to save their lives.

Some 'orphanages' are not content waiting for these kinds of opportunities to arise or for children to show up on their doorstep. They will send out a 'child-finder' or 'child-recruiter' to persuade parents of children in very poor and remote places to give up their children.[12] They make beautiful promises of full bellies, healthy children, good education and a bright future, to convince parents that it would be rather selfish to keep their child with them and deprive her of such opportunities. In some cases, these recruiters will even pay money to parents who are starving, to take their child to an 'orphanage' and a 'better future'.[13]

As with everything, in the 'orphanage industry' there are also places that are better than most and those that are worse than most. The degrees to which children are exploited and harmed varies. In some 'orphanages', children have been recruited and should not be there, but the people running the place are sincerely doing what they can to give the children a good life, even if institutional care will always fall short and they base everything on getting money from foreigners. There are also places, however, where the children are neglected because they are considered an unfortunate side-effect of making money from donations to orphans. Even worse, there are places where the people in charge have discovered that foreigners are even more willing to pay up if the situation looks bad, if the children are badly clothed and malnourished.[14] In these places, no matter how much money comes in through donations, the children are purposely kept badly dressed and malnourished to bring in even more money.[15]

That is an extremely harrowing thought, is it not? That your generous donations could actually be the cause of children being treated badly because it brings in more money.

The 'orphanage industry' does not limit itself to one type of income made from children in 'orphanages'. Other types include: Forced prostitution, both inside and around the 'orphanage', and after shipping children to other locations.[16] Children made to work or beg to bring in money.[17] The trafficking of children,[18] including trafficking in the form of adoption.[19] In countries like Nepal and Guatemala, the adoption programme has been shut down indefinitely because there were too many reports of children being sent abroad for adoption, while they were not at all available for adoption.[20] Parents enrolled their child in a cheap or free boarding school for education because no schooling was available in their remote village, only to find their child gone without a trace, with no documentation or information about where the child went, when they went to pick her up again. These children feel terrible, thinking that their parents have abandoned them and not understanding why they were suddenly sent away to a foreign country to live with strange people. Parents are looking for their children in desperation, without hope of finding them again. The adoptive parents on the other side have no idea where the child came from. They are not aware that the child is being trafficked. They presume they are doing a good thing by adopting a child who has no one else to care for her.[21]

Funding of 'orphanages' needs to be put to an end in order to stop all these kind of unscrupulous and unconscionable practices. The money can be put to so much better use.

---

1 Ghazal Kheshavarzian, Georgette Mulheir, Corinna Csaky (2015). *In Our Lifetime. How Donors Can End the Institutionalisation of Children.* Lumos, London; Georgette Mulheir, Kevin Browne (2007) *De-Institutionalisation and Transforming Children's Services. A guide to good practise.* European Commission Daphne Programme, UK p30

2 Kevin Browne (2009), *The Risk of Harm to Young Children in Institutional Care.* The Save The Children Fund, London p9

3 Eric Mathews, Eric Rosenthal, Laurie Ahern, Halyna Kurylo (2015) *No Way Home: The exploitation and abuse of children in Ukraine's orphanages* Disability Rights International USA p24; Unicef (2010) *At Home or in a Home? Formal care and adoption of children in Eastern Europe and Central Asia* Geneva, Switzerland p25

4 Bjarte Sanne (2008) *Understanding the Child. A mental needs manual for caretakers in children's homes 2nd Edition* p46

5 Corinna Csaky (2009) *Keeping Children out of Harmful Institutions. Why We Should Be Investing in Family Based Care* The Save The Children Fund, London p19

6 Ibid. p21

7 Unicef (2006) *Alternative Care for Children without Primary Caregivers in Tsunami Affected Countries. Indonesia, Malaysia, Myanmar and Thailand* UNICEF East Asia and Pacific Regional Office, Thailand p31-32 Ghazal Kheshavarzian, Georgette Mulheir, Corinna Csaky (2015). *In Our Lifetime. How Donors Can End the Institutionalisation of Children.* Lumos, London

8 Corinna Csaky (2009) *Keeping Children out of Harmful Institutions. Why We Should Be Investing in Family Based Care* The Save The Children Fund, London p21; Oliver Holmes (2016) *The Guardian:* 'Orphanage Tourism': fears of child exploitation boom as Myanmar opens up 29/09/2016; Georgette Mulheir, Mara Cavanagh (2016) *Orphanage Entrepreneurs: The Trafficking of Haiti's Invisible Children* Lumos Foundation p10; Unknown (2014) *Orphanage Trafficking and Orphanage Voluntourism. Frequently asked questions.* Next Generation Nepal p6-7

9 Ariel Carroll (2015) *Terms of Reference: Funding stream analysis of residential care* Elevate Children Funders Group

p2 Ghazal Kheshavarzian, Georgette Mulheir, Corinna Csaky (2015). *In Our Lifetime. How Donors Can End the Institutionalisation of Children.* Lumos, London

10 Corinna Csaky (2009) *Keeping Children out of Harmful Institutions. Why We Should Be Investing in Family Based Care* The Save The Children Fund, London p13-14; Georgette Mulheir, Kevin Browne (2007) *De-Institutionalisation and Transforming Children's Services. A guide to good practise.* European Commission Daphne Programme, UK p31

11 Ariel Carroll (2015) *Terms of Reference: Funding stream analysis of residential care* Elevate Children Funders Group p4; Georgette Mulheir, Mara Cavanagh (2016) *Orphanage Entrepreneurs: The Trafficking of Haiti's Invisible Children* Lumos Foundation

12 Corinna Csaky (2009) *Keeping Children out of Harmful Institutions. Why We Should Be Investing in Family Based Care* The Save The Children Fund, London p21; Oliver Holmes (2016) *The Guardian:* 'Orphanage Tourism': fears of child exploitation boom as Myanmar opens up 29/09/2016

13 Georgette Mulheir, Mara Cavanagh (2016) *Orphanage Entrepreneurs: The Trafficking of Haiti's Invisible Children* Lumos Foundation p10; Unknown (2014) *Orphanage Trafficking and Orphanage Voluntourism. Frequently asked questions.* Next Generation Nepal p6-7

14 Oliver Holmes (2016) *The Guardian:* 'Orphanage Tourism': fears of child exploitation boom as Myanmar opens up 29/09/2016

15 Ibid.; Unknown (2014) *Orphanage Trafficking and Orphanage Voluntourism. Frequently asked questions.* Next Generation Nepal p6;

16 Oliver Holmes (2016) *The Guardian:* 'Orphanage Tourism': fears of child exploitation boom as Myanmar opens up 29/09/2016; Eric Mathews, Eric Rosenthal, Laurie Ahern, Halyna Kurylo (2015) *No Way Home: The exploitation and abuse of children in Ukraine's orphanages* Disability Rights International USA p31, 52-56

17 Oliver Holmes (2016) *The Guardian:* 'Orphanage Tourism': fears of child exploitation boom as Myanmar opens up 29/09/2016

18 Corinna Csaky (2009) *Keeping Children out of Harmful Institutions. Why We Should Be Investing in Family Based Care* The Save The Children Fund, London p17-18

19 EveryChild (2012) *Adopting better care: Improving adoption services around the world.* EveryChild, London p15; Ghazal Kheshavarzian, Georgette Mulheir, Corinna Csaky (2015). *In Our Lifetime. How Donors Can End the Institutionalisation of Children.* Lumos, London p16; Unicef (2009) *Child-Trafficking in East and South-East Asia: Reversing the Trend* UNICEF EAPRO p11, 15

20 Kevin Voight, Sophie Brown (2013) *International Adoptions in Decline as Number of Orphans Grows* 17 September 2013, CNN, USA

21 Georgette Mulheir, Mara Cavanagh (2016) *Orphanage Entrepreneurs: The Trafficking of Haiti's Invisible Children* Lumos Foundation p10

What Can Be Done to Really Help?

All right, so we have established that giving money to children's homes is definitely not in the children's best interest. But now what? Does this mean we are just supposed to turn our backs on these children and let them rot in those children's homes while waiting for the people who try to make money over the backs of innocent children to realise that it is no longer profitable so they will stop recruiting children? No, of course not. There are definitely ways in which you can help children who are currently in children's homes and in which you can help prevent children from ending up in children's homes.[1]

To start with, if you are currently donating to a children's home, you could see if you can find out more about what kind of children they are helping and what they are doing for the children. Of course, when you ask people who run the children's home, you will get a beautiful story–a sales-pitch–but that can still give you quite a lot of information. If you ask directly whether the children still have living parents without giving an indication that there might be answers you would disapprove of, you will usually get an honest answer. It may be dressed up as 'Yes, but the parents are very poor and unable to feed the children' or 'Yes, but they live in a remote village where there is no school for the children to go to.' This way, you can get some kind of indication of whether this is a home for children who actually need someone outside of their family to care for them.

Next, you can try to get information on whether the people running the children's home are doing anything to make sure the children stay there for as short a time as possible. In some places, the children's home really only acts as a temporary, emergency solution, which may not be a terrible thing. Children who were found in the street or rescued from traffickers may stay there while information is found about parents or other relatives who might be able to care for them and much work may be put into reuniting family members. Or babies from single mothers who culturally have no way of keeping the baby and providing for it because they are outcast by the community might be taken in for a short while until a suitable adoption family is found. While it would be preferable to offer Mother-and-Baby homes (where mothers and babies are allowed to live together) in these cases, instead of just places where babies are to be abandoned, this may not always be feasible. If that is the case, it is worth continuing to support the organisation in the work they do to make sure that in the end, children are cared for in a loving family situation.

However, if the answers go in another direction and even though they are polished for marketing purposes seem to point towards the unsavoury situations that were described in the previous chapter, it might be a sign that you are better off not investing more money in that children's home because it will do more harm than good to the children. You can, of course, give the people running the place a second chance and see whether they are open to discussing ways in which to transform their 'orphanage' into something more beneficial to the children and the community. Checking whether or not they are open to such suggestions will give you a strong indication as to whether continuing to fund this particular children's home will be of benefit to the children.

A lot of suggestions can be made concerning what 'orphanages' could transform into to help make sure that more children are able to grow up in their own family and thrive there.[2] Just because children's homes are not the solution to the problem, does not mean that the people running such a home have nothing to contribute to the community. If they make a change, it should be something that is supportive of community life, rather than isolating children in an institution.[3]

The great news is that pretty much all alternatives to institutional childcare–including the still not ideal, but far, far better option of group homes–are much cheaper than the traditional orphanage setup.[4] Even directly handing out money to extremely poor parents to help them feed their children turns out to be cheaper than running a children's home.[5] Plus, most other options are easier to organise and to keep running smoothly than children's homes. Running a children's home, if done as well as can be done, is extremely complicated and expensive.[6] This is particularly good news because it means that by donating the same amount of money to a cause supporting community services, you can make an even greater impact in the lives of these children than you thought you could by donating to 'orphanages'.

I am familiar with one organisation that has started to make a change-over to being more supportive of families in the past few years, on their own initiative. The organisation has been running medical children's homes for many, many years. These are children's homes with exceptionally high standards of care, with a very low child-to-caregiver ratio, where a lot of attention and stimulation is provided to the children. They have also always only acted as a temporary home for children with complex medical needs from other children's homes. In this children's home, the children receive specialised medical care and money is raised to pay for surgeries and other hospital treatment if needed. Once the children are medically stable, they return to their original children's home or go into foster care. Over the years, the organisation has built up a reputation for being able to provide a high standard of special needs care, and sometimes they are contacted not by another children's home to see if they can take on a new case, but by a doctor at the hospital who is worried that the original children's home will not be able to provide the level of care needed by the child after surgery, for example. As this reputation grew, at times the organisation was contacted by doctors when there was a family with a child requiring surgery, who did not have the funds to cover the cost. The organisation would try to raise the funds to help out and make sure that the child could stay with their family. In recent years, this part of their operations has expanded. Now the organisation not only raises funds to help families pay for the medical procedures needed by their child, they also provide accommodation for poor families who have had to travel to the capital for medical treatment and have nowhere to stay. They provide help with making complicated medical decisions–if the family wants–and give training and guidance on the special care needed by the child after medical treatment, so that the family will be able to confidently handle the situation when they go home. If special medical supplies are needed and the family has difficulty to afford them, the organisation will do what it can to provide these too. This is an example of how a children's home can transition into a community service that helps keep families together.

So, what are the suggestions you could make to the children's home to have a more positive impact on the children's lives and do less harm? Here are some options, but it is by no means an exhaustive list:

- Turn into an organisation dedicated to reuniting street children, or those who are lost or trafficked, with their family.[7]
- Turn into an organisation that organises and supervises foster care for children who really have no one left to take care of them.[8]
- Turn into a community centre that provides support and guidance to parents who are struggling in some way.[9]
- Turn into an afterschool day-care programme, providing help with homework and tuition to children, also giving them a safe place to go when their parents are out working.
- Turn into a free school, so that children are able to have an education, even though they are from a poor family.
- Turn into a respite or day-care home instead of a children's home, allowing disabled children to get the specialised care and therapy offered in the 'orphanage' while still being able to live with their parents and receive their love. This also allows the parents to go to work, while their special needs child is safely cared for.[10]
- Set up a free healthcare clinic in the building, hiring doctors and nurses with foreign donations instead of using the money and the building for an 'orphanage'.
- Retrain 'orphanage' caregiving staff to

become foster parents, thereby providing a real home environment for the children who really have no one to look after them.

None of these change-overs are simple or straightforward, all of them require training and involvement from experienced people. However, making sure that experienced people are involved and that training is provided for staff, should also be the case when running a children's home. In almost all countries there are NGOs and government agencies that can help with the setting up or transformation of these kinds of services.

I would like to share the story of a suggestion I made in real life, along these lines.

> I got involved with a very large children's home where school-age children were cared for, many of whom were HIV-positive. They invited me to come visit them after I had made a proposal to change their children's home with a traditional orphanage setup to a group home setup. I explained that the group home setup would mean putting two adults in charge of set groups of no more than nine children, with each group living as an artificial family. This would make it a lot easier to meet the children's essential basic needs in the same way as in regular families.
>
> When I got to know the organisation running the children's home better, I started to change my mind about the best approach to help these children. First of all, I

learned that most of the children still had one or two living parents and that they were mostly in the children's home because their parents were struggling with their medical needs and found it hard to give them an education. Secondly, I discovered that the children's home was not the only project run by the organisation and that among the other projects, there was one that was particularly interesting. The organisation had started up small community centres in different slums in the area. In these community centres, after-school activities and tuition were organised for the children in the slum. They also held educational events for women and children, had built up a support network among the women, and organised free medical and dental check-ups from time to time. The children from the slum were picked up by the organisation's school bus and brought to the school at the children's home, which they got to attend for free, with uniforms and school materials all provided.

Meanwhile, it was becoming quite clear that the organisation was really struggling to meet the essential basic needs of the children in the children's home, despite their best attempts and intentions. On top of that, the transition from a traditional orphanage setup to a group home setup was being delayed further and further.

The combination of all these things eventually reached a point where I stopped pushing for the transition to group homes and started connecting the dots in my mind. I took a new proposal to the founder of the organisation: Instead of continuing to try and fail to properly care for the children in the children's home, would it not make much more sense to encourage the families to take the children back and then to provide them with support to enable them to cope with the things they were struggling with? I proposed to expand the community centre project a little by attaching a small health centre to each community centre. In this health centre, the organisation could hand out the ART medication that the HIV-positive children needed to take two or three times a day, and the regular follow-up visits and health check-ups needed by HIV-positive children could be arranged and coordinated from this place. By giving out ART medication, that burden was removed from the family. And by handing it out at set times, they could ensure that the medication was taken properly, something that is essential for ART to be effective and to avoid developing a resistance to it. Added to that, they could consider adding a kitchen and cooking one hot, healthy meal a day and serving it at a set time for dinner in the evening. This would serve two purposes at once: it would make sure that even the poorest children would at least get one nutritious meal a day, while the set timing of the dinner would make sure that there would be no problems with food being served at a time when children taking ART are supposed to have an empty stomach to make sure their medication works properly. In addition to these new services, the children could still be allowed to make use of the free school and school supplies and the free hospital attached to the children's home.

This is not the kind of change that gets made overnight and we are not there yet. But the suggestion was favourably received. Not least because organising the alternative is much easier to manage, logistically simpler and much cheaper than running a children's home.

As you see, there are many different options. If you are not already sponsoring a children's home and are looking for a way to help the most vulnerable children, sponsoring organisations involved in offering these kinds of community services is a good option. Likewise, if you happen to know someone who is planning to set up a children's home, you might be able to suggest to them that there are more effective and efficient options to help vulnerable children.

I did not want to include specific suggestions of organisations who need funds to help keep children out of children's homes–or in some cases to help get children out of children's homes–because there are so many worthy organisations, many of them only working at a local level. I am afraid that giving suggestions of certain organisations will make people think that these are more worthy or that others should be avoided, which is not true at all. No list I can give, could possibly be complete. However, I have been urged to give at least some examples. So I will, including the disclaimer that there are many other organisations out there doing great work.

Some large international organisations working to improve community services that help keep children out of institutions are:

- UNICEF
- Terre des Hommes
- Save the Children

- Lumos
- Doctors Without Borders
- Disability Rights International
- Oxfam
- CARE
- Children International

But please, also do your own research and find more organisations–particularly the local grass roots ones–to support.

To understand why these alternatives will help children come out of so-called orphanages and why they prevent them from ending up in one, we need to look at the reasons why most children end up in orphanages in the first place. It has already been mentioned that poverty (and the related inability to afford education) and disability are the main reasons, but they do not cover the whole story.[11] Poverty and disability do not make parents turn around and say: 'I don't want my child anymore, where can I drop her off?'

Poverty makes parents turn around and think: 'If I do not take that job, I cannot feed my child, but if I do take that job, my child will be by herself in the house all day long and that is not safe. What do I do now?' or 'I am not able to afford fuel for the stove and I am afraid that my child will freeze to death in the night. What do I do now?' or 'They tell me that the only way my child will have a better future than mine is if she learns to read and write in school, but I can only just afford to feed and clothe her, I cannot afford school fees and bus fees, I cannot buy a uniform or books. What do I do now?' or 'The last of the rice is gone, I can go without for a little while longer, but my child is so thin and so sick. What do I do now?'[12]

Having a child with special needs makes parents turn around and think: 'Could it really be true what the doctor said, that my child with Down's syndrome will never even know me anyway and that she will be better off if I just leave her in an institution? What do I do now?'[13] or 'How are we ever going to find the money to pay for the expensive surgery that my child needs to survive? What do I do now?' or 'How can I make the breathing equipment my child needs at night work, when we have no electricity in the house? What do I do now?' or 'The doctor said that my child will become seriously deformed if she does not get regular physiotherapy treatment, but it takes more than seven hours to travel to the city, where I can find a physiotherapist. What do I do now?' or 'It's great to see my child move around freely in that wheelchair through the smooth halls of the hospital, but how is she going to manage on the uneven tracks with all the holes and hills in the village? What do I do now?'[14]

Parents do not look for a way to get rid of their child, they look for a way to help their child, to save their child.[15] The problem occurs when while looking for help, they find none.[16] When there are no services available or affordable that allow them to provide their child with what she needs.[17] When for a while it seems like there is no answer and nothing can be done, and then… a solution presents itself. And it is that solution, which presents itself at that moment of desperation when no other solutions can be found, that makes everything so much worse.

The solution that presents itself is that there is free day care available, but only in combination with night care and weekend care. In other words: handing your child over to an 'orphanage', thinking that she will be better off because she will not be alone and neglected. The solution to hand over your child to an 'orphanage' where warm clothes, warm blankets and heating are provided, thinking that your child is now saved. The solution to hand your child over to an 'orphanage' where she will get free education, including a uniform, books and even tuition, thinking that your child is moving towards a bright future. The solution to hand your child over to an 'orphanage' where she will have her belly full all the time, getting several meals a day, thinking that now she will be able to grow up strong and healthy. Believing the doctor or community elder who says, against everything your instincts tell you, that your handicapped child will be better off and happier in a children's home. Not wanting to let go of your child, even though she has special needs, but loving her so much that you give her up so that she will be able to survive and get the most out of life, in a children's home.

Governments, unfortunately, also play a role in this situation. And again, it is despite their best intentions. Providing free education for orphans, free surgery for orphans or a monthly food allowance for orphans sound like beautiful, generous and charitable initiatives. It is great that orphans have these opportunities and benefits. However, where does that leave the poorest families? If they abandon their child, making sure that no one knows who her parents are, she will be registered as an orphan and if she goes to one of the 'orphanages' she will receive all of the things she needs, but not if she stays with her family. As long as she stays with her family, they have to provide for her, whether they are able to or not. And so, parents may feel like they do not have any other option but to abandon their child in order to give her the best possible chances in life.

This is why it is so essential that funding–from both governments and foreign donors–goes to a variety of community projects, allowing parents to access the services they need in order to be able to take care of their own children.[18] To make sure that parents are not forced to make these kinds of agonising decisions, in the hopes that they are giving their child a better future. When they look for help at a difficult time, they should see a selection of options open to them, none of which includes abandoning their child and having to live with the grief of having done that. Not to mention the fate that is in store for the child when she has to grow up in an institution that does not meet her essential basic needs and that will deny her the opportunity for normal growth and development. And that is not even taking into account the far greater risk of abuse and trafficking that she will be exposed to.[19]

This is why I write this book. I hope that by reading this, you become an ally in the fight for making sure children in institutions or at risk of ending up in institutions receive help and are protected from harm. And I hope that you will help me spread awareness about the evils of institutional childcare and the promising alternatives.

My dream come true would be to see institutional childcare a thing of the past in my lifetime. There are organisations working on it who claim that that can be done. In the meantime, I will stick with the motto that I have lived by for many years:

I cannot change the world, but I can change the world for one child. And then another. And another…

---

1 Ghazal Kheshavarzian, Georgette Mulheir, Corinna Csaky (2015). *In Our Lifetime. How Donors Can End the Institutionalisation of Children.* Lumos, London p19-20, 22, 31, 35-36 Unknown (2014) *Orphanage Trafficking and Orphanage Voluntourism. Frequently asked questions.* Next Generation Nepal p8

2 Unicef (2006) *Alternative Care for Children without Primary Caregivers in Tsunami Affected Countries. Indonesia, Malaysia, Myanmar and Thailand* UNICEF East Asia and Pacific Regional Office, Thailand p35-36

3 Corinna Csaky (2009) *Keeping Children out of Harmful Institutions. Why We Should Be Investing in Family Based Care* The Save The Children Fund, London p23

4 Georgette Mulheir, Kevin Browne (2007) *De-Institutionalisation and Transforming Children's Services. A guide to good practise.* European Commission Daphne Programme, UK p33; Georgette Mulheir, Mara Cavanagh (2016) *Orphanage Entrepreneurs: The Trafficking of Haiti's Invisible Children* Lumos Foundation p31; Maia Szalavitz (2010) How Orphanages Kill Babies -- And Why No Child Under 5 Should Be In One. *Huffington Post, 23 April 2010*; John Williamson, Aaron Greenberg (2010) *Families, Not Orphanages* Better Care Network p6-7; Ariel Carroll (2015) *Terms of Reference: Funding stream analysis of residential care* Elevate Children Funders Group p2

5 Oliver Holmes (2016) *The Guardian:* 'Orphanage Tourism': fears of child exploitation boom as Myanmar opens up 29/09/2016

6 Kevin Browne (2009), *The Risk of Harm to Young Children in Institutional Care.* The Save The Children Fund, London p6

7 John Williamson, Aaron Greenberg (2010) *Families, Not Orphanages* Better Care Network p16

8 Ibid. p17-18

9 Unknown (2005) *A Model for Community-Based Care for Orphans and Vulnerable Children. Nkundabana.* Care International Rwanda

10 Kevin Browne (2009), *The Risk of Harm to Young Children in Institutional Care.* The Save The Children Fund, London p19

11 Georgette Mulheir, Kevin Browne (2007) *De-Institutionalisation and Transforming Children's Services. A guide to good practise.* European Commission Daphne Programme, UK p24

12 John Williamson, Aaron Greenberg (2010) *Families, Not Orphanages* Better Care Network p14

13 Eric Mathews, Eric Rosenthal, Laurie Ahern, Halyna Kurylo (2015) *No Way Home: The exploitation and abuse of children in Ukraine's orphanages* Disability Rights International USA p28-29; Unicef (2010) *At Home or in a Home? Formal care and adoption of children in Eastern Europe and Central Asia* Geneva, Switzerland p31

14 Unicef (2010) *At Home or in a Home? Formal care and adoption of children in Eastern Europe and Central Asia* Geneva, Switzerland p33; Unknown (2014) Website: CRIN *DISABLED CHILDREN: The African Report on Children with Disabilities: Promising Starts and Persisting Challenges*

15 Ariel Carroll (2015) *Terms of Reference: Funding stream analysis of residential care* Elevate Children Funders Group p2

16 Eric Mathews, Eric Rosenthal, Laurie Ahern, Halyna Kurylo (2015) *No Way Home: The exploitation and abuse of children in Ukraine's orphanages* Disability Rights International USA p29

17 Unicef (2010) *At Home or in a Home? Formal care and adoption of children in Eastern Europe and Central Asia* Geneva, Switzerland p23 Ghazal Kheshavarzian, Georgette Mulheir, Corinna Csaky (2015). *In Our Lifetime. How Donors*

Can End the Institutionalisation of Children. Lumos, London

18 John Williamson, Aaron Greenberg (2010) *Families, Not Orphanages* Better Care Network p14

19 Kevin Browne (2009), *The Risk of Harm to Young Children in Institutional Care.* The Save The Children Fund, London p17; Corinna Csaky (2009) *Keeping Children out of Harmful Institutions. Why We Should Be Investing in Family Based Care* The Save The Children Fund, London p16-17; Oliver Holmes (2016) *The Guardian:* 'Orphanage Tourism': fears of child exploitation boom as Myanmar opens up 29/09/2016; Ghazal Kheshavarzian, Georgette Mulheir, Corinna Csaky (2015). *In Our Lifetime. How Donors Can End the Institutionalisation of Children.* Lumos, London p16; Eric Mathews, Eric Rosenthal, Laurie Ahern, Halyna Kurylo (2015) *No Way Home: The exploitation and abuse of children in Ukraine's orphanages* Disability Rights International USA p31, 35; Georgette Mulheir, Kevin Browne (2007) *De-Institutionalisation and Transforming Children's Services. A guide to good practise.* European Commission Daphne Programme, UK p30, p31-33; Georgette Mulheir, Mara Cavanagh (2016) *Orphanage Entrepreneurs: The Trafficking of Haiti's Invisible Children* Lumos Foundation p9; Unknown (2014) *Orphanage Trafficking and Orphanage Voluntourism. Frequently asked questions.* Next Generation Nepal p5; Unknown (2015) Website: CRIN *Mexico: Authorities Fail to Protect Children & Adults with Disabilities from Torture, Trafficking & Segregation*

References

Kevin Browne (2009). The Risk of Harm to Young Children in Institutional Care. The Save the Children Fund, London. <http://www.savethechildren.org.uk/resources/online-library/the-risk-of-harm-to-young-children-in-institutional-care> (29/04/2017).

Ariel Carroll (2015). Terms of Reference: Funding Stream Analysis of Residential Care. Elevate Children Funders Group. <http://elevatechildren.org/wp-content/uploads/sites/9/2015/06/ToR-Funding-stream-analysis-institutional-care.pdf> (29/04/2017).

Corinna Csaky (2009). Keeping Children out of Harmful Institutions. Why We Should Be Investing in Family-Based Care The Save the Children Fund, London. <http://www.savethechildren.org.uk/resources/online-library/keeping-children-out-of-harmful-institutions-why-we-should-be-investing-in-family-based-care> (29/04/2017).

EveryChild (2012). Adopting Better Care: Improving Adoption Services Around the World. EveryChild, London. < https://resourcecentre.savethechildren.net/sites/default/files/documents/6029.pdf> (05/06/2017).

Dr. Ronald S. Federici (1998). Institutional Autism. Help for the Hopeless Child: A Guide for Families. <http://drfederici.com/institutional-autism/> (22/05/2017).

Craig Haney, Curtis Banks, Philip Zimbardo (1973). Interpersonal Dynamics in a Simulated Prison. International Journal of Criminology and Penology 1973, 1, 69-97. California, USA. <http://pdf.prisonexp.org/ijcp1973.pdf> (29/08/2016).

Oliver Holmes (2016). 'Orphanage Tourism': fears of child exploitation boom as Myanmar opens up. The Guardian, 29/09/2016. <https://www.theguardian.com/world/2016/sep/29/orphanage-tourism-fears-of-child-exploitation-boom-as-myanmar-opens-up> (28/11/16).

Marinus H. van IJzendoorn, Marian J. Bakermans-Kranenburg (2003). Attachment Disorders and Disorganised Attachment: Similar and Different. Attachment and Human Development, vol 5, no 3, September 2003. <https://www.researchgate.net/profile/Marinus_Van_IJzendoorn/publication/10593338_Attachment_disorders_and_disorganized_attachment_Similar_and_different/links/0fcfd511231a5b86ba000000.pdf>(06/062017)

Ghazal Kheshavarzian, Georgette Mulheir, Corinna Csaky (2015). In Our Lifetime. How Donors Can End the Institutionalisation of Children. Lumos, London.

Florence Koenderink (2012). Children Everywhere. How to Provide Good Institutional Care to Infants and Toddlers. Book 1: Essential Elements of Childcare in Institutions. Orphanage Projects, Forfar.

Terry M. Levy, Michael Orlans (2000). Attachment Disorders as an Antecedent to Violence and Antisocial Patterns in Children. <http://www.hhs.csus.edu/sw/document/syllabus/fall%202008/sw224reader_gagerman.pdf> (30/10/2012).

Eric Mathews, Eric Rosenthal, Laurie Ahern, Halyna Kurylo (2015). No Way Home: The Exploitation and Abuse of Children in Ukraine's Orphanages. Disability Rights International, Washington, DC, USA. <https://www.driadvocacy.org/wp-content/uploads/No-Way-Home-final2.pdf> (29/04/2017).

Georgette Mulheir, Kevin Browne (2007). De-Institutionalisation and Transforming Children's Services. A guide to good practise. European Commission Daphne Programme, UK. <https://www.crin.org/en/docs/Deinstitutionaliation_Manual_-_Daphne_Prog_et_al.pdf> (29/04/2017).

Georgette Mulheir, Mara Cavanagh (2016). Orphanage Entrepreneurs: The Trafficking of Haiti's Invisible Children. Lumos Foundation, London. <https://wearelumos.org/sites/default/files/Haiti%20Trafficking%20Report_ENG_web_20EP16.pdf> (29/04/2017).

Bjarte Sanne (2008). Understanding the Child. A Mental Needs Manual for Caretakers in Children's Homes, 2nd Edition. <http://www.myanmarorphanages.com/wp-content/uploads/2012/11/Understanding-the-child-English-2nd-edition.pdf> (26/07/2015).

Maia Szalavitz (2010). How Orphanages Kill Babies–And Why No Child Under 5 Should Be in One. Huffington Post, 23 April 2010. <http://www.huffingtonpost.com/maia-szalavitz/how-orphanages-kill-babie_b_549608.html> (25/05/2011).

UNICEF (2015). Orphans. UNICEF. <https://www.unicef.org/media/media_45279.html> (27/02/2017).

UNICEF (2006). Alternative Care for Children Without Primary Caregivers in Tsunami-Affected Countries. Indonesia, Malaysia, Myanmar and Thailand. UNICEF East Asia and Pacific Regional Office, Bangkok, Thailand. <http://www.unicef.org/eapro/Alternative_care_for_children.pdf> (08/08/2015).

UNICEF (2009). Child-Trafficking in East and South-East Asia: Reversing the Trend. UNICEF East Asia and Pacific Regional Office, Bangkok, Thailand. <http://www.unicef.org/eapro/Unicef_EA_SEA_Trafficking_Report_Aug_2009_low_res.pdf> (08/08/2015).

UNICEF (2010). At Home or in a Home? Formal Care and Adoption of Children in Eastern Europe and Central Asia. Geneva, Switzerland. <http://www.unicef.org/

protection/Web-Unicef-rapport-home-20110623v2.pdf>
(01/08/2015).

Unknown (1948). Universal Declaration of Human Rights. <http://www.un.org/en/universal-declaration-human-rights/> (07/06/2017).

Unknown (1989). United Nations Convention on the Rights of the Child. <http://www.un.org/en/universal-declaration-human-rights/> (07/06/2017).

Unknown (2006). United Nations Convention on the Rights of Persons with Disabilities. <http://www.un.org/en/universal-declaration-human-rights/> (07/06/2017).

Unknown (2005). A Model for Community-Based Care for Orphans and Vulnerable Children. Nkundabana. Care International Rwanda, Kigali, Rwanda. <https://www.crin.org/docs/Rwanda%20Nkundabana.pdf> (06/08/2015).

Unknown (2014). Ending the Institutionalisation of Children Globally–The Time Is Now. Lumos Foundation, London. < https://wearelumos.org/sites/default/files/Ending%20Institutionalisation%20of%20Children.pdf> (29/04/2017).

Unknown (2014). Orphanage Trafficking and Orphanage Voluntourism. Frequently Asked Questions. Next Generation Nepal, Eugene, OR, USA. <https://www.crin.org/sites/default/files/next-generation-nepal_faqs-on-

orphanage-trafficking-and-orphanage-voluntourism.pdf> (05/09/2015).

Unknown (2014). Disabled Children. The African Report on Children with Disabilities: Promising Starts and Persisting Challenges. CRIN. <https://www.crin.org/en/library/publications/disabled-children-african-report-children-disabilities-promising-starts-and> (09/08/2015).

Unknown (2015). Mexico: Authorities Fail to Protect Children & Adults with Disabilities from Torture, Trafficking & Segregation. CRIN. <https://www.crin.org/en/library/publications/mexico-authorities-fail-protect-children-adults-disabilities-torture> (04/09/2015).

Kevin Voight, Sophie Brown (2013). International Adoptions in Decline as Number of Orphans Grows. 17 September 2013, CNN, USA. <http://edition.cnn.com/2013/09/16/world/international-adoption-main-story-decline/index.html> (06/06/2017).

Panayiota Vorria et al (2003). Early Experiences and Attachment Relationships of Greek Infants Raised in Residential Group Care. Journal of Child Psychology and Psychiatry 44:0 (2003), pp 1-13 <https://s3.amazonaws.com/academia.edu.documents/45399767/Early_experiences_and_attachment_relatio20160506-1071-7r3jh8.pdf?AWSAccessKeyId=AKIAIWOWYYGZ2Y53UL3A&Expires=1525002170&Signature=kId%2BQ8WfM6IQVDK5lL%2F1%2BZ182m8%3D&respon

se-content-disposition=inline%3B%20filename%3DEarly_experiences_and_attachment_relatio.pdf> (01/08/2017)

John Williamson, Aaron Greenberg (2010). Families, Not Orphanages. Better Care Network, New York, NY, USA. <http://www.bettercarenetwork.org/library/the-continuum-of-care/foster-care/families-not-orphanages> (29/04/2017).

www.ingramcontent.com/pod-product-compliance
Ingram Content Group UK Ltd.
Pitfield, Milton Keynes, MK11 3LW, UK
UKHW020220250726
13967UKWH00001B/99

9 780993 502330